Theories of Learning for the Workplace

Workplace and professional learning, lifelong learning, adult learning and learning in different contexts have become of more and more interest and now dominate all aspects of twenty-first-century life. Learning is no longer about 'storing and recall' but 'development and flow'.

Theories of Learning for the Workplace offers fascinating overviews into some of the most important theories of learning and how they are practically applied to organisational or workplace learning. With each chapter co-authored by an academic researcher and an expert in business or industry, this unique book provides practical case studies combined with a thorough analysis of theories and models of learning.

Key figures in education, psychology and cognitive science present a comprehensive range of conceptual perspectives on learning theory, offering a wealth of new insights to support innovative research directions.

Containing overviews of theories from Schön, Argyris, Senge, Engeström, Billett, Ericsson, Kolb, Boud and Mezirow, this book discusses:

- adult learning
- workplace learning
- informal learning
- reflective practice
- experiential learning
- deliberate practice
- organisational and inter-organisational expansive learning.

Combining theory and practice, this book will be essential reading for all trainee and practising educational psychologists, organisational psychologists, researchers and students in the field of lifelong learning, educational policy makers, students, researchers and teachers in vocational and higher education.

Filip Dochy is Professor of Research on Learning & Development and Corporate Training at the University of Leuven, Belgium. He is founding editor of the *Educational Research Review* and a member of the EARLI Executive Committee. He is also a Special Professor of Educational Innovation & IT at Maastricht University, the Netherlands.

David Gijbels is Assistant Professor of Learning and Instruction at the University of Antwerp, Belgium. He is Associate Editor of *Educational Research Review* and coordinator of EARLI's special interest group on Learning and Professional Development.

Mien Segers is Professor of Corporate Learning in the Department of Educational Research and Development at the Maastricht University School of Business and Economics, the Netherlands. She is also Series Editor for the EARLI book series, *New Perspectives on Learning and Instruction*.

Piet Van den Bossche is Assistant Professor at the University of Antwerp, Belgium, and at Maastricht University, the Netherlands.

Routledge Psychology in Education
Edited by Karen Littleton

The new *Routledge Psychology in Education* series is interdisciplinary in nature, publishing cutting-edge research in educational psychology and education-based research from related areas including cognition, neuropsychology and social psychology. Titles will take a broad and innovative approach to topical areas of research and will address the needs of both researchers and advanced students (Masters and Ph.D.) within both psychology and education programmes and related areas.

Titles in the series will:

- Review the field to provide an interesting and critical introduction for the student.
- Explore contemporary research perspectives, issues and challenges.
- Signpost future directions and trends.

Theories of Learning for the Workplace

Building blocks for training and professional development programmes

Filip Dochy, David Gijbels,
Mien Segers and
Piet Van den Bossche

Routledge
Taylor & Francis Group

LONDON AND NEW YORK

First published 2011
by Routledge
2 Park Square, Milton Park, Abingdon, Oxon OX14 4RN

Simultaneously published in the USA and Canada
by Routledge
711 Third Avenue, New York, NY 10017

Routledge is an imprint of the Taylor & Francis Group, an informa business

British Library Cataloguing in Publication Data
A catalogue record for this book is available from the British Library

Library of Congress Cataloging-in-Publication Data
Psychological theories of learning in the workplace / Filip Dochy . . . [et al.].
        p. cm.—(Routledge psychology in education)
    1. Employees–Training of–Psychological aspects. 2. Learning, Psychology of. 3. Adult learning. 4. Organizational learning.
    I. Dochy, F. J. R. C. (Filip J. R. C.)
    HF5549.5.T7P79 2012
    331.25′92019–dc22   2010051704

ISBN: 978–0–415–61893–9 (hbk)
ISBN: 978–0–415–61894–6 (pbk)
ISBN: 978–0–203–81799–5 (ebk)

Typeset in Galliard
by Keystroke, Station Road, Codsall, Wolverhampton

This book is dedicated to Professor Emeritus Herman Baert

Herman Baert is an expert in learning, professional development and HRD, and a well-respected researcher as well as one of the most inspiring teaching professors we have ever met. He is Professor Emeritus in Adult Education and Labour Pedagogy at the Catholic University of Leuven, Belgium.

Contents

Illustrations

Figures

Tables

Case studies

Introduction

Building training and development programmes on recent theories of learning

Filip Dochy

In current Bachelor and Master programmes in many disciplines – such as human resource development, psychology, business studies, economics, sociology, labour pedagogy, anthropology, medicine, teacher training, management programmes, leadership programmes, engineering, educational sciences, MBAs, learning sciences, etc. – research and theories on the workplace learning of professionals play a pivotal role.

The character of the book – reviewing the main theories and giving a voice to important researchers in the field – nicely addresses the needs of university professors, polytechnic teachers and students.

Research into learning and professional development has grown rapidly in recent years, and is still growing. Evidence for this is seen in the growth of the special interest groups in the European Association for Research in Learning and Instruction (EARLI) and in the American Educational Research Association (AERA), and also in communities of, for example, human resource development and vocational and educational training.

The state of the art is composed of a number of theories which have been developed after ongoing discussion. However, there is not yet available a comprehensive overview of these theories. This book provides such an overview and thus meets the current needs perfectly.

As all reviewed theories concern 'learning at the workplace' it can be said that this book is truly 'interdisciplinary' in nature. The origins of the different theories are diverse and range from strictly economic and management underpinnings, through cognitivist backgrounds to almost cultural-historical theoretical perspectives.

Whereas Peter Senge and Chris Argyris present their theories from a strongly business and management theoretical background, others such as Donald Schön start from an adult education perspective. Jean Lave is an anthropologist and social learning theorist, while Etienne Wenger has a background in computer sciences. Anders Ericsson is a cognitive psychologist and Yrjö Engeström is a psychologist specialising in adult education.

All the theories described in this book constitute necessary background knowledge for any professional engaged in training and development and interested in the development of training and learning programmes.

There is no strict order in the complexity of the consecutive theories presented in the chapters. However, the theories in the earlier chapters are not the most complex and are easier to explain and understand, while the last theory – Engeström's on inter-organisational expansive learning – is certainly the most complex. Engeström's theory is more abstract and more difficult to understand because it revolves around a higher level of learning within organisations (between units), or between organisations on the one hand, and the learning of knowledge that does not exist yet (knowledge that is developed during action, during the solving of the particular problem) on the other.

The interaction between the theories can be seen when one tries to put together a scheme that answers the following questions according to each theory: What are the core theoretical concepts? Who learns? Why do they learn? What do they learn? How do they learn?

A first attempt at putting together this scheme is presented below in Table 0.1. This scheme is certainly not definitive but its completion provides an interesting exercise for the reader in confronting theories as a basis for discussion.

To give the reader a good insight into each of the theories every chapter has an identical pedagogical arrangement: the chapter starts with a case captured from practice, followed by the explanation of the core theory and ending with an explicit application of the theory to the case, or an explanation of how the theory works or can be applied to the particular case. As such, all the theories can be applied to many other cases. We certainly urge readers, professors, teachers and students to try to apply the theories to other cases and to discuss in small groups whether these applications seem to be appropriate.

Table 0.1 Theories of learning

	Core issues/concepts	Who learns?	Why do they learn?	What do they learn?	How do they learn?
Billett and Ellstrom The learning curriculum; workplace learning	• the 'experienced' curriculum • individual contribution • workplace environment • participation • guidance (direct and indirect)	• individuals, and therefore organisations	• to remain up-to-date • growth & development • employability • to resolve non-routine problems	• competence • employable outcomes • qualifications • interactions that learners engage in are central to what they learn	• participation/ engagement in enacting a personal curriculum (pathway of engagement in activities) • personal ontogenies • guidance (direct/ indirect) • creative learning
Mezirow Transforma-tional/ transformative learning	• transformative/ transformational learning • experience • critical reflection • development • learning as a meaning-making activity (meaning schemes, meaning perspectives)	• individuals	• disorienting dilemma • disruption of their world view	• new meaning perspectives • to become more reflective, critical and open	• making meaning/ interpretation • critical reflection • discourse • action • perspective transformation

Table 0.1 Continued

	Core issues/concepts	Who learns?	Why do they learn?	What do they learn?	How do they learn?

Kolb and Boud Experiential Learning Theory	• experiential learning
	• experience
	• learning styles
		• individuals	• conflict
			• differences
			• disagreement
				• creation of knowledge
				• to relearn ideas/ beliefs
					• grasping/ transforming experience:
					  – concrete experience
					  – reflective observation
					  – abstract con-ceptualisation
					  – active experi-mentation

Lave and Wenger Situated learning	• situated learning • LPP • community of practice • social nature of learning/ contextualised	• members of a community of practice • newcomers and old-timers	• to develop skills and knowledge • to get full membership • to handle creative problem-solving	• construction of identities/ personality skills	• participating in community of practice – observing, working together/sharing with experienced workers • LPP

Senge Systems thinking theory	• learning organisation
	• fifth discipline
	• strategy
	• principle of leverage
	• limits to growth
		• individuals and therefore organisations	• individual and business growth
			• to stay competitive
				• to become healthy, successful learning organisations
				• changes in thinking
				• to manage change
					• five building blocks:
					  – system thinking
					  – personal mastery
					  – mental models
					  – building shared vision
					  – team learning

Theory	Key concepts	Actors	Aims		Process
	• shifting the burden • systems thinking • shared vision • team learning (mental models)				• alter limiting factors
Argyris and Schön Organisational learning	• organisational learning • reflection-in-action • reflection-on-action • theories of action (espoused theory and theory-in-use) • single loop learning • double loop learning	• individuals • organisations	• to survive in an ever-changing environment • to become reflective practitioners	• to challenge assumptions • to construct new descriptions/re-frame • to find solutions	• single-loop/model I • double-loop/model II • reflection
Engeström Expansive learning and inter-organisational learning	• expansive learning • activity theory • contradictions • knotworking and boundary crossing • co-configuration • multi-voicedness • historicity • change laboratory	• parties engaged in activity systems • organisations (inter-organisational learning)	• contradictions • double bind	• new forms of work activity • what is not there yet	• cycle of expansive learning: – questioning – analysing – modelling – implementing – reflecting – consolidating

Chapter 1

Deliberate practice, the high road to expertise: K. A. Ericsson

Margje W. J. van de Wiel, Piet Van den Bossche and Richard P. Koopmans

Case study: the case of medical specialist training

Medical doctors start their training after finishing secondary school. In the Netherlands, medical studies are organised according to the bachelor-master scheme. The training takes six years: a three-year bachelor programme with mostly theoretical studies, followed by a three-year master phase in the hospital. After six years of successful study the student is licensed as an MD, and takes the oath. However, independent work as a medical doctor is not yet possible, because the Dutch government has put in place a law that more or less obliges all doctors to do some sort of specialist training after graduation.

Approximately 2,800 students start their medical studies every year. After graduation, approximately 1,000 of these continue for specialist training, which usually takes four to six years, and approximately 600 continue their training to become general practitioners (GPs), which takes three years. This postgraduate training phase is usually spent as a doctor working in the training area, either a hospital or a GP practice, and the students are normally closely supervised by senior practitioners. Hereafter, we will mainly consider medical specialists who work in hospitals only.

A usual day in such a training programme is spent as follows. The trainee, also called a resident, is allocated to an in-patient ward, the outpatient ward, the emergency ward or a treatment area (e.g., the operating room). Depending on what stage the student has reached in his or her training there may be a supervisor physically present. However, particularly in such medical specialisms as internal medicine, the supervisor is often not physically present but will be readily contactable by phone. Residents see approximately 10 to 20 patients on such a day. They are in close contact with other residents at all different stages of training, as well as with undergraduate students. They work closely together with all sorts of paramedics, especially nurses, whom they instruct on the approach to be taken for the individual patients. Residents assume responsibility for the actions taken, which they share with their supervisors. There is a grey area between actions which are largely the responsibility of the residents and those for which supervisors are mainly responsible. Residents are in regular contact with their supervisors during the day, usually for short discussions (e.g., one to five minutes) on how to proceed with individual patients.

How does learning take place in such a training programme? Much learning is implicit in such a training programme. That is, residents observe others taking certain actions and receiving feedback on the proposed management plan from their supervisors. From this they construct for themselves what is the most appropriate action to be taken in a given case. There is usually no explicit check that residents have deduced the correct instructions from these observations and feedback. However, over the years of training residents will have many different supervisors and will work in many different hospitals; therefore over time and with experience students will come to understand the most appropriate courses of action that would be approved by their supervisors. In recent years an emphasis has been put on more explicit learning, i.e., taking courses in certain subjects, usually not in the workplace itself, and taking exams that test both knowledge and practical skills. Moreover, in the workplace there will be everyday meetings that will contribute to residents' learning on the job.

These meetings touched on above are usually patient-centred, with the aim of discussing patients' conditions and the actions to be taken, proposed by a resident among a group of other residents and supervisors. There are daily morning sessions in which the night-shift doctors hand over their work, and daily ward rounds in which residents discuss with nurses and with their immediate supervisors the patients on their ward. Every week, there are so-called grand ward rounds in which an extended group of residents, medical staff, nurses and other paramedics review the patients on their ward. Usually, there are also weekly meetings to discuss particular issues, such as pathology reports and radiology results, and meetings with specialists about special problems, such as oncology cases. In most of these meetings residents are expected to present a case and to propose the actions to be taken in patient care.

During their medical training residents have to sit a number of written examinations, usually on the subject of their chosen specialism. Often this is a formative assessment and the results do not influence graduation. Most judgements on the progression of residents are subjectively made by the group of supervisors. They give their overall impression of the behaviour of a resident in the workplace and usually take into account both specialism-related skills, such as skills demonstrated in the operating room, and more general skills, such as communication with patients. In recent years some emphasis has been put on structured observation of residents. For such an observation a supervisor will typically observe residents for 15 minutes, score an Objective Structured Clinical Examination (OSCE) form and give some feedback. Such forms have also been developed for practical skills. The number of such structured observations is limited; typically some 10 to 20 have to be done annually to comply with official regulations.

During recent years there has been a lot of discussion on this type of learning in practice. Several issues have been put forward in such discussions. A main theme is the way in which residents receive feedback on their work, and the quality of this feedback. In programme evaluations, residents often indicate that they want more feedback. According to some authorities both the quality and quantity of feedback should be improved. Another theme is the implicit learning, in which the learning climate is a major issue; today there are even scoring forms on which residents can score the quality of their learning climate. The issue here is whether learning during specialism training is facilitated or not; so, do the supervisors allocate time to answer questions? How is the caseload? How do the supervisors deal with stressful situations? And so on. The main question here is to what extent residents can learn from their daily work. Another theme is what residents should learn on simulators, and what they should learn from working with actual patients. Patient safety is of course important, but residents who have had a relatively small caseload during their training might be unfit to work independently after graduation. A further issue concerns in what settings residents should do their training, and whether the mix of cases they encounter can be adjusted to facilitate learning. As residents mainly see the patients that are either staying on the ward in which they work or are visiting the hospital outpatient ward, the cases they are confronted with depend on the type of patients that are hospitalised or visit the outpatient ward. In a university hospital residents might see many very special cases that they will probably never see again in their later practice, while in a non-university hospital residents might see many more routine cases. Another theme that is currently influencing learning is the working-time direc-tive. At present, the working hours of residents have been limited to approximately 50 hours per week. For reasons such as shift-working, but to some extent also because of obligations to do courses, part-time working arrangements, pregnancy (more than 50 per cent of residents are women) and vacations, residents have very irregular working weeks. A perceived problem in this respect is that residents often cannot see the outcomes of their actions, as they will only be caring for a certain patient for a short time.

Introduction

Professional expertise is based on a large and well-organised knowledge base that is developed in great part by learning from experience. Based on his research on workplace learning Eraut (2000) has stressed the importance of this non-formal learning during work; most human learning does not occur in formal contexts such as schools, courses and training, but in everyday contexts. In describing a typology of non-formal learning, Eraut pointed to the level of intention to learn as a fundamental distinction. On the one hand, there is implicit learning, in which there is no intention to learn and no awareness of the learning process. On the other hand, learning can be deliberative: it is planned, and time is specifically set aside. A category between these two types of learning has been described as reactive. This learning takes place in response to specific situations and events that draw attention. This near spontaneous and unplanned learning can vary in level of intentionality.

Theories on the development of expertise are traditionally based on differences in performance as a result of experience emphasising the role of implicit learning to tune knowledge to its practical use (Chase & Simon, 1973; Ericsson & Lehman, 1996; Norman, Eva, Brooks, & Hamstra, 2006). However, the deliberate activities that could be undertaken by professionals to learn from their experiences must also be taken into account. The theory of deliberate practice (Ericsson, Krampe, & Tesch-Römer, 1993) addressed this last aspect, arguing that mere practice is not enough to attain expertise but that focused efforts are needed.

This chapter presents the theory of deliberate practice. Based on the description in the case study of the professional learning environment in which physicians are trained, we will discuss how deliberate practice theory can inform the development of this environment so that expertise is fostered.

The theory of deliberate practice

Extensive practice and experience in a professional domain is, according to deliberate practice theory (Ericsson et al., 1993; Ericsson, 2004, 2006, 2009), important but not sufficient to reach expert levels of performance. With this theory, the nature of the practice activities engaged in plays a decisive role in the development of expertise. It is argued that practice activities contribute most if they are specifically designed and structured to develop performance aspects that need improvement and if they allow feedback and repetition. This so-called deliberate practice requires the motivation to improve performance and to engage in sustained efforts to refine knowledge and skills. It also requires sufficient resources in terms of the time and energy that can be spent on training, as well as in terms of the access to teachers, coaches, training material and facilities that support and enable learning. On the path to excellence, trainers and coaches have an important role in guiding training and the learning process. They analyse performance, plan and design the practice activities and monitor performance to provide informative feedback and to adjust training methods and strategies. With this individualised supervision they help the performer to attend to critical aspects of performance and to focus on knowledge of results so that effective self-monitoring during independent practice is enhanced. Experts in a domain have gradually learned to control, monitor and evaluate their performance themselves and try to find the best possible methods and teachers to further improve.

Research on deliberate practice has mostly been done in competitive domains, such as music, chess and sports (Ericsson, 2006, 2009). In line with the monotonic benefits assumption it has been found that the amount of time an individual has engaged in deliberate practice activities is directly related to that individual's level of performance (Charness, Tuffiash, Krampe, Reingold, & Vasyukova, 2005; Ericsson et al., 1993; Ward, Hodges, Williams, & Starkes, 2004). The higher the investment in deliberate practice, the better the performance is. The type of practice that has the largest impact on the acquisition of expertise, however, differs across domains. In music and chess, accumulated and current amount of practice alone has been found to be the major determinant of expert performance (Charness et al., 2005; Ericsson et al., 1993). Piano players, for example, practice music pieces over and over again guided by the feedback of their teachers, steadily building up a repertoire of more complex pieces by working on their technique and expression. Chess players study published games and reflect on the best next move for each position and compare their prediction to the move by the master. In sports, the deliberate practice activities that best predict top-level performance are sport specific (Ward *et al.*, 2004). For individual sports like figure skating or swimming, practising the tasks that needed to be performed at competitions contributed most. For team sports, however, the amount of engagement in team practice discriminated between players' skill levels. In soccer, for example, players need to practice technical mastery and strategic insight to optimally cooperate during a match. This domain-specificity of relevant practice activities stresses the importance of analysis for training design by selecting the most representative tasks of the domain that need to be improved.

Becoming an expert takes a long time of effortful engagement in deliberate practice. The general rule is that at least ten years of practice are required to attain expertise (Ericsson *et al.*, 1993). This is much more than is needed to accomplish a complex skill such as driving a car, which most people can master in less than 50 hours. Skill acquisition research has shown that, according to the power law of practice, a performance asymptote can be reached within a manageable time period for most daily skills and laboratory tasks (Anderson, 1981; Fitts & Posner, 1967). Therefore, Ericsson (Ericsson *et al.*, 1993; Ericsson, 2006, 2009) distinguished deliberate practice to reach expertise from the mere repetitive practice that has been described in this traditional skill acquisition research to result in increases of speed and accuracy and eventually in fully automatic behaviour. Ericsson also made a clear distinction between deliberate practice and experience. Having experience in a domain does not necessarily mean that one has reached full mastery of the relevant tasks. For example, an amateur chess player may have been actively involved in the game for as many years as a master player but for fewer hours and in a different way. Experience within a domain without receiving feedback and making adjustments in behaviour may even lead to learning inefficient or inaccurate routines. The central thesis of deliberate practice theory is that skilled performance and experience are not enough to acquire superiority in a domain, and that automaticity should be counteracted by achieving high-level control of performance that allows further improvements to be made (Ericsson, 1998, 2004, 2006, 2009).

The cognitive mechanisms that mediate expert performance have been described as complex integrated systems of mental representations (Ericsson, 2004, 2006, 2009). Based on a highly developed network of knowledge and skills, experts in a field have accurate and precise representations of the current situation and task, their goals and the ways in which they might achieve these goals. These representations enable them to perform the task proficiently and at the same time monitor and adjust performance whenever necessary. They also use these representations to evaluate their performance afterwards and to retrieve associated representations in their knowledge base when reflecting on the outcomes. In chess, for example, masters have stored a huge number of chess game representations in their memory that they use in weighing up the best next move and envisioning the consequences of more and less favourable moves. The conclusions of the evaluation and reflection processes, as well as the feedback received, are used to fine-tune the system of representations. These are, in turn, the starting point for the planning of subsequent learning and practice. Experts are continuous learners who never seem satisfied, but want to perfect their performance and always try to improve on their current level.

This last characterisation of experts sharply contrasts with the motivation and possibilities of most professionals working in organisations. The primary task of these professionals is to complete job-related tasks on time, while often only few resources are available to reconsider their work and assess their developmental progress. According to Ericsson (2004, 2006, 2009) most professionals reach an acceptable level of performance during the initial phase of their career and then stay at this level without serious attempts to develop beyond the proficient execution of routine tasks. Only some individuals surpass this level and succeed in their continuous efforts to develop themselves as they become recognised as outstanding professionals in their domain. Research on deliberate practice in the workplace, however, is limited. The few studies carried out related to the fields of education (Dunn & Shriner, 1999), insurance (Sonnentag & Kleine, 2000) and organisational consultancy (Van de Wiel, Szegedi, & Weggeman, 2004), and looked for activities that are performed with the aim of learning or improving professional competence. The work-related activities identified as deliberate practice in these work settings are preparation, mental simulation, asking for feedback or advice, evaluation, reflection and updating activities. These activities closely resemble key elements of self-regulated learning, in which individuals plan, monitor and reflect on their learning to optimise the outcomes (Van de Wiel et al., 2004; Zimmerman, 2006). However, engagement in deliberate practice was certainly not common, as professionals were usually involved in these activities to reach their work-related goals. In their study, Sonnentag and Kleine showed that insurance agents who handled more cases and were more engaged in deliberate practice yielded better sales performance. According to Van de Wiel et al., more time was spent on deliberate practice if an organisation structurally implemented procedures that promoted cooperation, evaluation and research in multidisciplinary teams.

Recently, research on deliberate practice in the workplace was extended to the medical domain (Van de Wiel, Van den Bossche, Janssen, & Jossberger, 2010), demonstrating that most work-related learning activities were directly related to patient care rather than motivated by competence improvement goals. Physicians were primarily concerned with their patients and sought advice and feedback when necessary to provide high-quality health care. The standards they used to evaluate their performance were tied to patients' conditions. With respect to their professional development they particularly valued the patients encountered and the discussions with colleagues about patients, as well as involvement in teaching and keeping up to date. These results indicate that much could be gained from managing learning opportunities in clinical practice more explicitly. Similar conclusions were drawn from reviews of expert performance in medicine and nursing (Ericsson,

2004; Ericsson, Whyte, & Ward, 2007) that advocated a deliberate practice approach for training these professionals. Measurement of performance is crucial in such an approach in order to detect individual shortcomings, generate immediate feedback and guide training design to achieve reproducible superior performance. Computer programs or simulators providing repetitive practice of relevant tasks that increased in complexity were found to be particularly appropriate for this. Another advantage of such programs is that learners may be confronted with unfamiliar situations and are allowed to make mistakes and learn from them. However, to enhance performance in daily practice, the learning outcomes of such training need to be transferred and sustained in the workplace, and an active attitude towards learning during regular work should be promoted. Work experiences that were proposed to contribute to the diagnosis and treatment of patients included specialisations by seeing more patients with similar diseases, accurate feedback by using sophisticated diagnostic equipment, interaction with knowledgeable colleagues, involvement in teaching and supervision and contribution to active research programmes.

Guiding principles for developing expertise based on deliberate practice theory

From the descriptions of deliberate practice, the cognitive mechanisms by which expert performance is developed and the resources required to engage in deliberate practice, recommendations can be deduced for designing learning environments that promote the acquisition of expertise. We formulated seven principles guiding the development of expertise:

- Principle 1: Informative and immediate feedback is fundamental in order to refine knowledge and skills.
- Principle 2: Measuring and analysing current performance is the cornerstone to improving it.
- Principle 3: Practice activities need to be specifically designed to improve performance aspects that need improvement.
- Principle 4: Practice activities need to be repetitive but also allow for reflection on outcomes and processes.
- Principle 5: The motivation to improve performance is a prerequisite to achieving expertise.
- Principle 6: Time and effort need to be invested.
- Principle 7: Teachers and coaches play a crucial role in guiding individual development.

Reflection on training practices in medicine from a deliberate practice perspective

The description of medical specialist training in the case presented above clearly showed that residents mainly learn on-the-job to become a registered professional in their field of specialisation. This embedding of learning in clinical work might be an asset as medical practice provides abundant meaningful learning opportunities that are by definition representative of the tasks to be performed. However, the focus on practising medicine does not allow for extended efforts on specific learning activities as advocated by deliberate practice theory. Major challenges for developing professional expertise, therefore, lie in better exploiting learning opportunities during daily work and balancing learning on- and off-the-job. Based on the guiding principles for developing expertise derived from deliberate practice theory, we will reflect upon the described training practices in hospitals and provide recommendations for improvement. We will begin our analysis with learning from feedback, as obtaining relevant information on one's performance in medical practice is a prerequisite to improving it. Subsequently, we will discuss the evaluation of performance, which may considerably contribute to generating useful feedback. We will continue with an analysis of the learning resources available and the practice activities that may be undertaken. We will then address residents' motivation and effort to learn. Finally, we will reflect upon the teaching and coaching role of the supervising medical staff.

Learning from feedback

During their work residents may obtain useful feedback on their performance from several sources. The three major sources are the patients' clinical condition, the people they work with or consult and the patients themselves. In diagnosing and treating a patient residents have to obtain a clear representation of the patient's problem by gathering information through history taking, physical examination, laboratory tests and additional tests like X-rays or CT-scans. The information they successively acquire in diagnostic and treatment processes can be regarded as feedback on the developing case representations and the actions taken. This feedback processing requires analytical effort in diagnostic reasoning, which has been described as the generation and testing of hypotheses, and is especially pertinent to difficult cases (Elstein, 2009; Elstein & Schwarz, 2002). When residents are not certain of what is wrong with a patient, such a systematic approach to problem-solving, in which relevant alternatives are examined and weighed up, contributes to the building of their knowledge base. The feedback present in the evolving condition of the patient, as substantiated by clinical examination, allows the fine-tuning of residents' knowledge that underlies their further reasoning. However, residents and experienced physicians do not usually regard this type of information as feedback, although they use it in patient monitoring and management and value it to assess their diagnosis and treatment (Van de Wiel, Van den

Bossche *et al.*, 2010). Higher awareness of the role of this information in expertise development and more effort and opportunity to follow-up on patients, are needed to enhance reflection on the course of disease and the decisions made. This implies that the fragmentation of duties in residents' current work schemes needs to be reconsidered. Natural occasions for reflection on patient cases, such as handovers and handoffs, may also be utilised for that purpose.

Supervisors, other medical specialists, fellow-residents, nurses and paramedics are also important sources for providing performance feedback. While working with a resident in patient care, they can form an impression of the resident's knowledge, skills and attitudes by discussing the proposed management plans and observing behaviour. According to deliberate practice theory, feedback on task performance should be given immediately, directed at those aspects that need to be improved and informative as regards the way of adjustments. Such feedback might be most feasible for well-defined tasks and technical skills. In discussing patients, however, the exchange of knowledge and information focuses on deciding on the best possible care for the patient rather than on the resident's professional development. Critically questioning the rationale of the actions proposed by residents, explaining suggestions for changes in approach and checking residents' understanding further contributes to refining the knowledge that directs their future performance. In the same way, feedback on the manner in which residents deal with patients and their families, colleagues and students may help them to communicate more effectively and to promote cooperation.

A third source of feedback that is hardly used, but might be easily tapped in hospitals, is the experience of patients. Patients can provide direct feedback on how they feel they have been treated. They know whether they were well informed about the disease process, the diagnostic actions, the treatment and their possible consequences; whether this information was clearly communicated; and whether they felt listened to. Patient feedback could be more systematically used as an information source by inviting patients to talk about their experience in the hospital. This takes some extra time, but provides information on how patients perceive their complaints, their disease process, possible complications, the received care and the communication with and among health professionals.

Providing and receiving feedback on performance might be difficult. To be most effective, it needs to be directed at the task and the learning process and not at the person him- or herself as this may invoke defensiveness rather than learning (Kluger & DeNisi, 1996; Watling & Lingard, 2010). This is in line with the recommendation that for deliberate practice immediate and specific feedback on task performance must be provided that aims for improvement. As feedback also needs to be tailored to the residents' cognitive level, it is required to assess their case representations as well as their underlying knowledge and skills. To facilitate the appropriateness of feedback, residents may play an active role in seeking it. They have responsibilities towards patients and are in charge of their own learning processes. Therefore, they need to regularly check whether their thinking about patients is in agreement with those of their supervisors, and whether their attitudes towards patients are valued or could be improved. In an open atmosphere consultation with specialists is common when problems are encountered (Van de Wiel, Van den Bossche *et al.*, 2010). However, the recognition of potential problems requires the accurate monitoring of uncertainty in medical decision-making and the accurate assessment of one's own knowledge and skills. This is not self-evident as has been shown in self-assessment research (Davis, 2009; Eva & Regehr, 2005, 2008). At the very least, residents should ask for advice when they feel uncertain. Therefore, they need to give priority to performance improvement and set aside ego and image defence considerations (Ashford, Blatt, & VandeWalle, 2003). This might be easier in situations involving high risks or uncertainty such as in health care, in which feedback has a high instrumental value (i.e., preventing patient harm and promoting patient safety), as well as in supportive environments in which feedback-seeking and discussion are encouraged (i.e., fine-tuning of case representations and treatment plans with supervisors) (ibid.).

Performance evaluation

The measurement of performance is crucial in a deliberate practice approach to expertise development. To improve on current levels of performance, it has to be determined what this current level is, what superior performance entails and how the gap between those two can be bridged. In medicine this might be feasible for well-defined tasks and routine clinical cases for which the more experienced and recognised specialists agree what should be done. For these cases, practice guidelines based on clinical research are usually available. However, in many cases the application of guidelines to individual patients is not straightforward as clinicians need to integrate information on a patient's condition, preferences and behaviour (e.g., compliance to drug intake) with the best evidence (Davis, 2009; Sackett, Rosenberg, Gray, Haynes, & Richardson, 1996). In particular, in the more complex and rare cases for which expert thinking and action are required, objective performance standards are rather problematic and a 'gold standard' based on measured superior performance is missing (Ericsson, 2004). In these cases, clinicians have to make decisions under uncertainty and discuss diagnostics and management plans within a team of professionals that are knowledgeable about the patient and the related areas of disease in order to find the best practices. The outcomes then generate feedback to evaluate the decisions made. For the evaluation of residents' performance this means that multiple measures need to be used to assess their knowledge and skills, as well as their ability to manage uncertainty and self-regulate their learning.

The case description showed that while performance standards are often implicit in the feedback given and the actions taken by supervisors, how residents internalise this information is not explicitly checked other than by what they show in subsequent performance. To increase transparency of the standards used and the rationale behind them, starting the discussion of these standards among specialists and residents is needed. A more precise and detailed set of performance criteria in different areas of competence (e.g., medical diagnosis and patient communication) allows us to pinpoint weak and strong aspects of performance and, hence, steer learning efforts. In this way, the clinical supervisors evaluating the progression of residents can go beyond the global judgements based on their overall impressions and provide more informative feedback. The same is true for residents themselves in assessing their performance and how to improve it. Formative knowledge tests and structural observations of clinical examination and practical skills certainly are an important step in setting and communicating performance standards. However, as these planned assessments occur only one or two times per month and are performed by only a single rater per observation, their scope is limited to representing residents' performance in a particular situation at a given moment. The challenge is to integrate assessments of performance, knowledge, skills and attitudes as the basis for feedback within daily work routines to ensure both residents' development and patient safety. Therefore, the supervising medical staff could more systematically apply direct observation of behaviour, probe residents to verbalise their thinking processes and ask questions to gain further insight into their case representations, underlying knowledge and uncertainties (Bowen, 2006). These point-of-care assessments of residents' competence would also provide insights into which areas a resident can work in independently and, hence, need less supervision in (Kennedy, Regehr, Baker, & Lingard, 2008). Research on this issue in internal medicine and emergency care (ibid.) showed that supervisors most often assessed residents' trustworthiness by double-checking the results of their clinical assessments and by the way in which they present a patient's case. They wanted to be confident that in dealing with patients residents had the relevant knowledge and skills, were conscientious in data gathering and came to ask for help when they were not sure. This last point shows that it is also important to assess how residents monitor and control their performance.

Learning resources and practice activities

Obviously the most restricted resource within the on-the-job medical specialist training is the time available and taken for developmental purposes. As patient care is the primary concern and often demands the resident's full attention, learning is largely a by-product of clinical work. If more time can be spent on assessing the way residents engage in this care, and on discussing points of improvement, they will learn more from their daily experiences. Therefore, work practices need to be scrutinised to see how time can be freed up for learning.

Other important resources in this on-the-job learning context are the patient cases encountered and the procedures that need to be performed. These cases and procedures largely determine what is practised and what can be learned, while their frequency and order cannot be planned as in designing deliberate practice. Questions raised in this respect in the example of medical specialist training concerned the number and type of cases that need to be seen in order to master a domain (respectively referred to as caseload and case mix) and, hence, permit independent practice. If individual assessments by residents and their supervisors may lead to some regulation of the cases to be dealt with and the skills to be practised, time could be devoted to those aspects that provide most learning opportunity. For example, routine cases and procedures could be delegated to less experienced residents, medical students or paramedics, whereas specific practice activities could be arranged to discuss the more complex cases that are not often seen but contribute to the development of a balanced knowledge base. For some skills, training efficiency might be increased by implementing repetitive practice with immediate feedback in specific training settings or simulators. Best practices in patient care and new developments in the field may be efficiently dealt with by specialists in courses designed for residents or continuing medical education. Guided by the assessment of residents' knowledge and skills, the balance between learning on- and off-the-job needs to be carefully sought so that what has been learned can be applied within medical practice. To enhance the transfer of training to the workplace, the format of training, further opportunities for practice and supervisor support are critical (Blume, Ford, Baldwin, & Huang, 2009; Davis, O'Brien, Freemantle, Wolf, Mazmanian, & Taylor-Vaisey, 1999).

To increase learning from experience, work-related activities that contribute to learning could be further exploited and promoted. Meetings in which patients are discussed have a high learning potential as they require the building of shared case representations by exchanging information and knowledge, problem-solving and decision-making within a group of professionals with different expertise and roles. Learning from these meetings may be increased by giving more emphasis to the educational function, activating residents' thinking by the use of critical questions, explaining considerations underlying decisions and checking for shared under-standing (Van de Wiel, Hanssen, Hendriks, Bauhüs, Philippens, & Koopmans, 2010). If this was done consistently in these meetings and in individual supervision, automaticity in reasoning may be counteracted and knowledge structures adapted. Knowledge may also be refined by elaborating case discussions with mental simulations of possible scenarios and comparing and contrasting patient features, diagnoses and treatments (Bowen, 2006). Furthermore, the acts of seeking feed-back and advice in case of uncertainty, systematic reflection, teaching, explaining and keeping up to date need to be encouraged in order to create a learning climate that fosters professional expertise.

Motivation and effort to learn

The motivation to improve performance is a prerequisite for deliberate practice. In the education and training literature this motivation is known as a mastery goal orientation and has been shown to be positively related to self-regulated learning and performance (Payne, Youngcourt, & Beaubien, 2007; Pintrich, 2000). This means that learners who want to master a topic and improve their knowledge and skills take control over their own learning and are able to plan, monitor and reflect on their actions to achieve their goals (Pintrich, 2000; Zimmerman, 2006). As described in deliberate practice theory, it is important to set specific challenging goals to direct the learning process (Latham & Pinder, 2005). Less favourable for learning are a performance approach goal orientation in which learners want to prove and compare competence to others, and a performance avoidance goal orientation in which they avoid failure and negative judgments (Payne *et al.*, 2007; Pintrich, 2000). Research on this topic in medicine found that although residents' mastery goal orientation was consistently higher than their performance goal orientation, a higher performance goal orientation was associated with higher perceived costs of feedback seeking (Teunissen, Stapel, van der Vlueten, Scherpbier, Boor, & Scheele, 2009), and a performance avoidance goal orientation with shunning differences of opinion (Van de Wiel, & Van den Bossche, 2008) and the seeking of both self-validation and self-improvement information (Janssen & Prins, 2007). These results indicate that a safe environment in which residents can openly discuss what they do not know and are not sure of is needed to increase efforts for learning. Residents themselves should be fully aware that they are in training and will progress faster when they invest in building their knowledge and skills.

Teaching and coaching

The supervising medical staff play a significant role in guiding residents' development. They (need to) set the standards, evaluate performance, provide feedback, engage in teaching dialogues to refine residents' knowledge, skills and attitudes, arrange practice activities and create a supportive learning environment. A review of the clinical teaching literature showed that good teachers are thought to foster positive relationships in an open atmosphere, encourage participation, activate critical thinking and show enthusiasm for the profession, in addition to their mastery of technical skills and medical knowledge (Sutkin, Wagner, Harris, & Schiffer, 2008). Moreover, the supervising specialists are the role models that residents observe. The way they behave sets the norms and values for professional conduct in a department. They not only demonstrate how to perform procedures and apply their knowledge in clinical reasoning, but also show whether it is acceptable to share uncertainty, seek further information, feedback, advice and explanation, think aloud and exchange arguments in discussion, and be critical in trying to achieve the best results for patients and to improve competence. As coaches they need to focus on the progress of individual residents. And it is the responsibility of the management team to consider what measures can be implemented to enable clinicians to fulfil their roles as model, teacher and coach.

Conclusions

This chapter highlights that from deliberate practice theory useful guiding principles can be derived to analyse the learning of professionals in the workplace and to come up with recommendations to promote the acquisition of expertise. For the training of medical specialists we suggest that the quantity and quality of feedback could be enhanced by more systematic use of the available resources, more reflection and discussion about performance standards guiding feedback, and an active attitude of residents to share their concerns and uncertainties in a safe and supporting environment. The adjustment of work schemes may allow for individual practice and patient follow-up. Learning from experience can be further enhanced by capitalising on the exchange of knowledge and experience in daily work routines. The close monitoring of residents' performance and progress can guide specific practice activities for those aspects that need improvement. Both residents and supervising medical staff need to be aware of the described learning processes and methods, so that they might be better able and more committed to invest in the development of knowledge, skills and attitudes. Finally, the organisation has a role in promoting and facilitating work and training procedures that enable both high-quality patient care and expertise development.

References

Anderson, J. R. (1981). *Cognitive skills and their acquisition*. Hillsdale, NJ: Lawrence Erlbaum.

Ashford, S. J., Blatt, R. & VandeWalle, D. (2003). 'Reflections on the looking glass: A review of research on feedback-seeking behavior in organizations', *Journal of Management*, 29(6), 773–799.

Blume, B. D., Ford, J. K., Baldwin, T. T., & Huang, J. L. (2009). 'Transfer of training: A meta-analytic review', *Journal of Management*, 36(4), 1065–1105.

Bowen, J. L. (2006). 'Educational strategies to promote clinical diagnostic reasoning', *New England Journal of Medicine*, 355(21), 2217–2225.

Charness, N., Tuffiash, M., Krampe, R., Reingold, E., & Vasyukova, E. (2005). 'The role of deliberate practice in chess expertise', *Applied Cognitive Psychology*, 19(2), 151–165.

Chase, W. G., & Simon, H. A. (1973). 'Perception in chess', *Cognitive Psychology*, 4, 55–81.

Davis, D. (2009). 'How to help professionals maintain and improve their knowledge and skills: Triangulating best practices in medicine', in K. A. Ericsson (ed.), *Development of professional expertise: Toward measurement of expert performance and design of optimal learning environments* (pp. 180–202). New York: Cambridge University Press.

Davis, D., O'Brien, M. A. T., Freemantle, N., Wolf, F. M., Mazmanian, P., & Taylor-Vaisey, A. (1999). 'Impact of formal continuing medical education: Do conferences, workshops, rounds, and other traditional continuing education activities change physician behavior or health care outcomes?', *Journal of the American Medical Association*, 282(9), 867–874.

Dunn, T. G., & Shriner, C. (1999). 'Deliberate practice in teaching: What teachers do for self-improvement', *Teaching and Teacher Education*, 15(6), 631–651.

Elstein, A. S. (2009). 'Thinking about diagnostic thinking: A 30-year perspective', *Advances in Health Sciences Education*, 14(Suppl 1), 7–18. Digital Object Identifier 10.1007/s10459-009-9184-0.

Elstein, A. S., & Schwarz, A. (2002). 'Clinical problem solving and diagnostic decision making: Selective review of the cognitive literature', *British Medical Journal*, 324, 729–732.

Eraut, M. (2000). 'Non-formal learning and tacit knowledge in professional work', *British Journal of Educational Psychology*, 70, 113–136.

Ericsson, K. A. (1998). 'The scientific study of expert levels of performance: General implications for optimal learning and creativity', *High Ability Studies*, 9(1), 75–100.

Ericsson, K. A. (2004). 'Deliberate practice and the acquisition and maintenance of expert performance in medicine and related domains', *Academic Medicine*, 79(Suppl 10), S70–81.

Ericsson, K. A. (2006). 'The influence of experience and deliberate practice on the development of superior expert performance', in K. A. Ericsson, N. Charness, P. J. Feltovich & R. R. Hoffman (eds), *The Cambridge handbook of expertise and expert performance* (pp. 683–704). New York: Cambridge University Press.

Ericsson, K. A. (2009). 'Enhancing the development of professional performance: Implications from the study of deliberate practice', in K. A. Ericsson (ed.), *Development of professional expertise: Toward measurement of expert performance and design of optimal learning environments* (pp. 405–431). New York: Cambridge University Press.

Ericsson, K. A., & Lehman, A. C. (1996). 'Expert and exceptional performance: Evidence of maximal adaptations to task constraints', *Annual Review of Psychology*, 47, 273–305.

Ericsson, K. A., Krampe, R. T., & Tesch-Römer, C. (1993). 'The role of deliberate practice in the acquisition of expert performance', *Psychological Review*, 100(3), 363–406.

Ericsson, K. A., Whyte, J., & Ward, P. (2007). 'Expert performance in nursing: Reviewing research on expertise in nursing within the framework of the expert-performance approach', *Advances in Nursing Science*, 30(1), E58–E71.

Eva, K. W., & Regehr, G. (2005). 'Self-assessment in the health professions: A reformulation and research agenda', *Academic Medicine*, 80(10), S46–S54.

Eva, K. W., & Regehr, G. (2008). '"I'll never play professional football" and other fallacies of self-assessment', *Journal of Continuing Education in the Health Professions*, 28(1), 14–19.

Fitts, P., & Posner, M. I. (1967). *Human performance*. Belmont, CA: Brooks/Cole.

Janssen, O., & Prins, J. (2007). 'Goal orientations and the seeking of different types of feedback information', *Journal of Occupational and Organizational Psychology*, 80(2), 235–249.

Kennedy, T. J. T., Regehr, G., Baker, G. R., & Lingard, L. (2008). 'Point-of-care assessment of medical trainee competence for independent clinical work', *Academic Medicine*, 83(Suppl 10), 89–92.

Kluger, A. N., & DeNisi, A. (1996). 'Effects of feedback intervention on performance: A historical review, a meta-analysis, and a preliminary feedback intervention theory', *Psychological Bulletin*, 119(2), 254–284.

Latham, G. P., & Pinder, C. C. (2005). 'Work motivation theory and research at the dawn of the twenty-first century', *Annual Review of Psychology*, 56, 485–516.

Norman, G. R., Eva, K., Brooks, L., & Hamstra, S. (2006). 'Expertise in medicine and surgery', in K. A. Ericsson, N. Charness, P. J. Feltovich & R. R. Hoffman (eds), *The Cambridge handbook of expertise and expert performance* (pp. 339–354). New York: Cambridge University Press.

Payne, S. C., Youngcourt, S. S., & Beaubien, J. M. (2007). 'A meta-analytic examination of the goal orientation nomological net', *Journal of Applied Psychology*, 92(1), 128–150.

Pintrich, P. R. (2000). 'The role of goal orientation in self-regulated learning', in M. Boekaerts & P. R. Pintrich (eds), *Handbook of self regulation* (pp. 451–502). San Diego, CA: Academic Press.

Sackett, D. L., Rosenberg, W. M., Gray, J. A., Haynes, R. B., & Richardson, W. S. (1996). 'Evidence based medicine: What it is and what it isn't', *British Medical Journal*, 312, 71–72.

Sonnentag, S., & Kleine, B. M. (2000). 'Deliberate practice at work: A study with insurance agents', *Journal of Occupational and Organizational Psychology*, 73(1), 87–102.

Sutkin, G., Wagner, E., Harris, I., & Schiffer, R. (2008). 'What makes a good clinical teacher in medicine? A review of the literature', *Academic Medicine*, 83(5), 452–466.

Teunissen, P. W., Stapel, D. A., van der Vleuten, C., Scherpbier, A., Boor, K., & Scheele, F. (2009). 'Who wants feedback? An investigation of the variables influencing residents' feedback-seeking behavior in relation to night shifts', *Academic Medicine*, 84(7), 910–917.

Van de Wiel, M., & Van den Bossche, P. (2008). 'Deliberate practice in medicine: Activities and attitudes at the workplace and their relation to expertise. Paper presented at the Symposium on Advances in Medical Expertise and Other Knowledge Intensive Working Environments, 4–6 June, Centre for Learning Research, University of Turku, Finland.

Van de Wiel, M. W. J., Szegedi, K. H. P., & Weggeman, M. C. D. P. (2004). 'Professional learning: Deliberate attempts at developing expertise', in H. P. A. Boshuizen, R. Bromme, & H. Gruber (eds), *Professional learning: Gaps and transitions on the way from novice to expert* (pp. 181–206). Dordrecht: Kluwer.

Van de Wiel, M. W. J., Van den Bossche, P., Janssen, S., & Jossberger, H. (2010). 'Exploring deliberate practice in medicine: How do physicians learn in the workplace?', *Advances in Health Sciences Education*, 16, 81–95. Digital Object Identifier 10.1007/s10459-010-9246-3.

Van de Wiel, M., Hanssen, C., Hendriks, R., Bauhüs, V., Philippens, J., & Koopmans, R. P. (2010). 'Physicians' learning through information and knowledge sharing in patient review meetings'. Paper presented at the 5th EARLI Learning and Professional Development SIG Conference, 25–27 August, Munich, Germany.

Ward, P., Hodges, N. J., Williams, A. M., & Starkes, J. L. (2004). 'Deliberate practice and expert performance: Defining the path to excellence', in A. M. Williams & N. J. Hodges (eds), *Skill acquisition in sport: Research, theory and practice* (pp. 231–258). London: Routledge.

Watling, C. J., & Lingard, L. (2010). 'Toward meaningful evaluation of medical trainees: The influence of participants' perceptions of the process', *Advances in Health Sciences Education*. Digital Object Identifier 10.1007/s10459-010-9223-x.

Zimmerman, B. J. (2006). 'Development and adaptation of expertise: The role of self-regulatory processes and beliefs', in K. A. Ericsson, N. Charness, P. J. Feltovich & R. R. Hoffman (eds), *The Cambridge handbook of expertise and expert performance* (pp. 705–722). New York: Cambridge University Press.

Chapter 2

Workplace curriculum: practice and propositions

Stephen Billett

Case study: a personal perspective on the workplace curriculum

This chapter describes and elaborates on the concept of the 'learning curriculum' as a means of organising and enacting learning experiences in practice settings (e.g., workplaces). My own personal curriculum – path that I have run – offers an illustration of this concept. The occupation I initially trained in was as a clothing technician and designer for the menswear manufacturing industry. In the early 1970s, I attended a college in Manchester in England, full time over a period of two years, to learn my occupational skills. During that time, I engaged in classes that taught me about pattern-making, textiles, garment design, manufacturing and the operation of production processes and clothing manufacturing equipment, etc. Over this two-year period, I can only recall visiting a clothing factory once, and that was for a brief walk through a large manufacturing plant where hundreds of women were manufacturing men's suits.

I did quite well at college and won a medal for getting the highest score nationally in the external examinations (i.e., City and Guilds of London Institute) associated with my course. So, I had a comprehensive college preparation and had excelled within that environment and with its measures of performance. Yet, despite such success, and having participated in a course specialising in my intended occupation, upon leaving college and starting work in my first job in the clothing industry, I found it difficult to relate most of what I had learnt to what was occurring and was required of me in this workplace. Quickly, I came to believe that my college preparation had done little to assist me in being effective within this workplace. The physical environment was different to anything I had previously experienced, the pattern-making was a particular house style based around well-proven precedents, but different from those I knew, the design process was restricted to a few individuals, and not myself, and the process of manufacturing was quite remote from anything I had previously experienced. Consequently, I experienced what many others have encountered in the transition from college to work: a form of dissonance between the experiences in the educational and the practice setting. Yes, the company manufactured mainly women's garments, but I had studied the construction of women's garments, although preferring menswear. Essentially, I struggled to carry forward what was learnt in the college environment and processes to this workplace. The point here is that the educational provision, even for a high achiever, had not enabled the translation or transfer of knowledge from the circumstances in which it was learnt to another set of circumstances. It seemed that it was more my diligence as a worker, rather than my college-based preparation, that secured me some successes in that workplace.

My second job in the clothing industry was with a large and quite high-quality menswear manufacturer, which was closer to where my family lived. In this company, which was owned by Quakers, I was employed as an assistant designer working in the design department, where patterns were made and arrangements for garment production were organised. Yet, it was in this workplace that I encountered a model of occupational development that was very well organised, and its processes and outcomes had a powerful impact upon my subsequent career in the clothing manufacturing industry, and maybe beyond.

More recently, drawing upon the work of the anthropologist Jean Lave (1990) I have come to refer to this process as the workplace curriculum or learning curriculum. Initially, working in the pattern-making room my activities were restricted to preparing and cutting out interlining patterns. These are the components which are adhered to cloth for particular strengthening purposes. The key requirement was that they had to be positioned about a centimetre inside of the cloth components to which they were adhered. My supervisor showed me how to use the pattern shears and gave me parameters within which to work. That is, all of the pencil line had to be on the waste card and the component parts had to be at least a centimetre in from the cloth components. Doing this task repeatedly, I developed not only accuracy but also smoothness in pattern cutting and an ability to cut out intricate shapes quickly. Then, I was permitted to cut out lining patterns (i.e,. the components which sit inside jackets and waistcoats), before being allowed to cut out patterns for cloth components. Those familiar with Lave's (ibid) work on apprenticeships in tailoring in Liberia will see many similarities here.

However, this pathway of preparation was not restricted to the design room. After being in the workplace for a few months, and proving my worth as a diligent and hard-working employee, I was given a remarkable learning opportunity, although I did not necessarily realise or appreciate it at the time. I was sent to work in the manufacturing lines. This clothing manufacturing company produced trousers, waistcoats and jackets both as mass-manufactured items and also as garments made for individual orders. For the next three months or so, I would spend every day in the production lines working on clothing manufacturing equipment, mainly straight sewing machines, and working my way through each of the three production lines. First, I worked in the trouser plant learning how to over-lock components and learn to do so with increasing accuracy and speed. Again, I was given, first, components to make, on which if I made a mistake the consequences could be limited. My pathway of progress through the plant began with making belt-loops, then pocket components, assembling pockets, waistband construction, under-pressing, making and inserting fly openings, seaming, pressing, hemming and final pressing. Second, I progressed to the waistcoat plant learning a different range of manufacturing tasks and skills including making welt pockets, the assembly of straps, lining backs and fronts, bagging-out waistcoats, under-pressing and finishing front edges, and inserting buttonholes and attaching buttons with a button sewing machine, among many others. Many of the skills here were distinct from those in the trouser plant and introduced me to a different form of garment construction where the entire garment needed to be finished and lined. From here, and finally, I went to work on the jacket production line which included assembling linings, components or pockets and facings, making pockets, assembling fore-parts and sleeves, assembling the body components, different kinds of under-pressing, including shaping shoulder seams and fine front edges, inserting sleeves and preparing sleeve crowns, then collars and on to finishing off jackets by sewing on buttons and making buttonholes, etc.

At the time, I felt quite ambivalent about being asked to work on the production line, although I came to enjoy it and learned a lot about the skills of people who are often referred to dismissively as production workers. But more than this, there was a series of significant legacies for my skill development that arose from these experiences which were quite profound and, in many ways, emulated what I was supposed to learn in the college programme: adaptable knowledge. Of course, I learnt a whole range of very specific procedures (e.g., particular operations) that were important for my career because of my understanding of how these procedures could be used to manufacture garments. I also learnt how to use a range of sewing machines very effectively. But, more strategically, I learnt about the sequencing of garment manufacturing, a range of critical considerations for production, and the roles and requirements of specific pieces of equipment and how they could be utilised and adapted for particular purposes.

All of these were powerful learning outcomes for me, and were strategic in nature. These outcomes were very helpful in this particular job and in my subsequent career within manufacturing, and also later on when I became a vocational teacher of garment design and manufacture. Subsequently, I found that very few people in garment manufacturing understood the entire garment-making process, and particularly in ways that permitted them to solve problems outside of their own specific areas of knowledge. However, most of these people had not had the opportunity of a college preparation, and even fewer had been fortunate enough to have the kinds of workplace preparation that I had enjoyed: through the pathway of experiences in the workplace described here.

Introduction

As indicated above, this chapter describes and elaborates on the concept of the 'learning curriculum' as a means of organising and enacting learning experiences in practice settings (e.g., workplaces). It does this by identifying how the concept of organising learning experiences arises through both the imperatives of practice settings and their goals, but also through elaborating on how these experiences have important pedagogic qualities. Drawing upon ideas that arose from anthropological studies (e.g., Lave, 1990) about how learning is organised in settings where occupational practices are enacted, a theory of organising and enacting the learning practice is discussed and detailed. In all, it is proposed that although curriculum needs to be considered in personal terms, the organisation of experiences in a practice setting can be organised and enacted in ways that can enhance both individuals' engagement and learning. The chapter began with an account of experiences, or a personal curriculum in educational institutions and workplaces, that were formative in developing my occupational skills as both a clothing technician and also as a vocational educator. In some ways, these experiences established my interest in and understanding of the worth of organising and sequencing these experiences to secure better learning outcomes, and also the importance of viewing the curriculum as something that individuals experience. Following on from here is an elaboration of the concept of the learning curriculum as articulated by Lave (ibid.) that is subsequently discussed as being a legitimate model of curriculum and the means for progressing the development of professional capacities in workplace settings. This elaboration of the learning curriculum includes a consideration of the identification of and engagement with richly pedagogic activities in workplace settings.

Learning at the workplace

If we take its original meaning, a curriculum is nothing other than a certain sequencing of experiences in which learners engage: a course to be run (Marsh & Willis, 1995). Yet, perhaps most often, curriculum is seen as being something quite different than this. It is commonly seen as a set of experiences that are organised and that are the result of deliberations involving a range of stakeholders and consideration of perspectives about what should be learned and through what means that learning should proceed. These deliberations then often result in sets of goals, processes, identified content and intended outcomes, usually captured in a document (i.e., a syllabus or course outline). Consequently, curriculum is often seen as being that which is intended, usually by others than those who teach or who are to learn (e.g., students) yet who have significant and particular interests in how what they intended is enacted in educational institutions (Quicke, 1999). Less often referred to is the idea of the 'experienced curriculum' – what students experience and construct (i.e., learn) from what has been organised and enacted. From the perspective of individuals' learning, but not always from the perspective of educational provisions, the 'experienced' curriculum is the most salient curriculum concept. This is because this concept is about the learning that occurs and arises through experiences provided for or engaged with by learners. In this conception of curriculum, individuals' personal developmental histories or ontogenies (Scribner, 1985) play key roles in how they construe and construct what they experience. Hence, the particular set of experiences students or other learners have when engaged in an educational programme or workplace situation can be seen as being part of the pathway along which they are progressing and which is likely to be person dependent in some way. They are engaged in enacting a personal curriculum. Consequently, and given the nature and character of the experienced curriculum (i.e., what learners experience and construct), it is clear that this concept of curriculum cannot be constrained to what occurs in educational institutions. This is because students, apprentices, novices or learners have experiences across a range of settings, which contribute to their ongoing development across their life histories or ontogenies. Likely, these individuals' experiences within educational institutions are not easily separable from other kinds of experiences (Bloomer & Hodkinson, 2000; Hodkinson & Bloomer 2002; Hodkinson, Billett, & Bloomer, 2004). For instance, whether referring to trades' apprentices or novice practitioners in professions, they are also likely to have engaged in significant experiences within practice settings, as well as those in educational institutions. Collectively, it is these experiences which constitute a personal curriculum: a track of experiences which is probably unique in some way to the individual. The processes of construing and constructing those experiences are person dependent (Valsiner, 2000).

Following on from the above, in considering how the development of professional capacities have or should be developed it is essential to go beyond viewing learners' curriculum as being that which is provided through educational institutions alone. Further, and in particular, when considering an educational project that intends to develop occupational or professional capacities it is important that experiences in workplace settings and how these relate to experiences within the educational setting, are considered. With the realisation in recent decades about the importance of the contributions of the social and physical world to individuals' learning (Brown, Collins, & Duguid, 1989; Rogoff, 1990; Salomon, 1997), and a realisation that the kinds of activities and interactions that learners engage in are central to what they learn (Rogoff & Lave, 1984), there has also come a reconsideration of the worth and legitimacy of experiences in workplace settings. Yet, regardless of whether the consideration is about one or the other or even both educational and workplace settings, it is important for the perspectives and pathways of the individuals who are positioned as learners to be included. Lest we forget, it is these individuals who actually engage in the process of learning and, by degree, respond (i.e., construe and construct) to what others intend and organise for them (Billett, 2009a). Hence, there is the need to consider personal pathways.

However, here the discussion is very much about the concept of the learning curriculum: a set of experiences that are provided for learners in the practice setting. Therefore, having provided this introduction to the concept of a learning or workplace curriculum, it is now necessary to discuss the origins of this approach to the organisation of learning and also identify some of its key attributes.

The learning curriculum

Proposed above is the idea that concepts of curriculum are often associated with institutional purposes (e.g., schools or schooling systems). Indeed, some of the early definitions arising through the discipline of curriculum studies emphasised curriculum as being about achieving the purposes of schools (Marsh & Willis, 1995; Skilbeck, 1984). Similarly, the anthropological accounts that are the sources of the concept of the learning curriculum also emphasise the achievement of the learning required to engage in, remake and sustain either the community or the cultural practice in which the individual is being engaged. Pelissier (1991) illuminates the processes by which individuals come to engage with a cultural practice and learn through participation in that practice, usually in the absence of direct instruction, or anything which resembles the process of teaching occurring in contemporary educational institutions. There are exceptions, such as when the knowledge to be learnt is not accessible and, therefore, artefacts (e.g., shells on a beach) are used to assist the learning of a skill which is important to a cultural practice (e.g., navigating at night by fishermen). These anthropological studies also remind us that across human history the vast majority of learning for occupational practices has occurred through participation in those practices. Indeed, it is only in the last century that the learning of occupational skills has increasingly moved into provisions within educational institutions (Billett, 2010). Up until relatively recently, the only occupations that were prepared within educational institutions were the key professions (Bennett, 1938; Greinhart, 2002; Wall, 1967/1968).

So, the processes of learning through practice and the organisation of experiences in workplaces to develop the kind of occupational skills which both individuals and enterprises need have long been enacted in workplaces, and perhaps most commonly within family and the family business (Lodge, 1947). Yet, because of the growth of provisions within specialised vocational education institutions across advanced industrial economies over the last hundred years or so, it might be commonly accepted that the provision of initial education for occupations is best done in such institutions, and that the learning arising through those provisions is inherently superior and more organisable than those in workplace settings. Even if these premises were correct, there is much to question in them. For instance, developments in understanding how people come to learn (i.e., construct knowledge) are increasingly emphasising that the key focus needs to be on the learners, and that the kind of experiences that are provided for learners will have significant impacts upon their learning (Brown *et al.*, 1989; Collins, Brown, & Newman, 1989; Fuhrer, 1993). Moreover, and perhaps in response to criticisms of the shortcomings of substitute environments such as those provided in educational institutions, there has been an increasing emphasis on providing learners with experiences that are authentic in terms of the capacities aiming to be developed through educational and development programmes (Billett, 1993; Billett, 2006; Gott, 1989; Greeno, 1989; Palinscar & Brown, 1984; Raizen, 1991). Also, and more pragmatically, across both higher education and vocational education systems in countries with advanced industrial economies have come demands for programmes to be directly related to occupational outcomes and for students to be 'job ready' on graduation (Australian Industry Group, 2007; Bailey,

Hughes, & Moore, 2004; Billett, 2009b; Department of Innovation, 2008; Universities Australia, 2008). Consequently, there has been a growing interest in students engaging in workplace activities from governments, educational institutions, teachers and also from students themselves who are increasingly seeking to secure employable outcomes through their personal and financial investment in their tertiary education.

Yet, underlining pragmatic agendas addressing concerns about the applicability of knowledge arising from experiences solely based in education institutions are the emerging understandings about learning highlighted above. That is, a focus on individuals' engagement and socially rich and authentic experiences. First, both individually and socially oriented constructivist accounts emphasise the active process of meaning-making that individuals engage in. It is not surprising that there has been an increasing emphasis on human dispositions, interest, learner agency and engagement in recent theorizing (Billet, 2006; Cho & Apple, 1998; Hodkinson & Hodkinson, 2004; Perkins, Jay, & Tishman, 1993; Tobias, 1994). Second, the interest in engagement in socially rich and authentic experiences has also led to interest in the processes of participation in social practices and the establishment of the metaphor that links participation and learning (Hodges, 1998; Sfard, 1998). These kinds of considerations then lead to considering curriculum not as being something which is the sole province of educational institutions, but as something cast more broadly within social and cultural practices and which accommodates individuals' processes and trajectories of participation within those practices, such as the learning curriculum.

It is noteworthy that the pathway constituting the curriculum that Lave (1990) identified is analogous to the original meaning of the term curriculum: *currere* – 'the track to be run', the course of learning (Marsh & Willis, 1995). In an anthropological account of learning through participation in practice, the curriculum or course of learning is not presented as a set of subjects that are to be successfully completed as in educational institutions. Progression here is premised upon the successful completion of subsequent subjects. Instead, a sequence of tasks to be successfully learnt and practised is the foundation for this conception of curriculum. Progression requires successfully learning and practising these tasks on the way to learning to perform more complex and demanding tasks that are central to the continuity and survival of the community (Pelissier, 1991) or workplace. The imperative here is for the sequencing of activities that workers progress along to secure the continuity of the work practice (i.e., the enterprise's goals, or those of cliques and affiliates in workplaces) through participants' learning, and their remaking of that practice as they engage with new tasks and workplace challenges. These imperatives likely take two forms: first, the need to develop the kinds of skills that the enterprise requires to function effectively to survive and prosper; and, second, developing these skills in ways that do not jeopardise the enterprise's continuity.

Although not stated in the form of a syllabus, the norms that shape these pathways operate in similar ways to a syllabus: setting out the activities, goals to be achieved and means by which progress and attainment can be secured. As proposed in Lave's (1990) study, tailors' apprentices learn by participating in workplace activities sequenced to provide engagement in tasks of increasing accountability and complexity. This pathway of engagement in activities progressively provided access to learning the capacities required for the work being undertaken in the particular tailors' workshops. The apprentices' initial activities were structured to provide access to the workplaces' goals and performance requirements for particular tasks. Initially, the apprentices engaged in finishing and ironing completed garments. Participation in these tasks afforded opportunities for the apprentices to understand the garment components; what a finished product looked like. This included the standard of finish demanded for garments within this workshop. These experiences presented the apprentices with observable and explicit goals for their performance of these tasks and those in which they would soon engage. Following this, the apprentices learnt specific procedures for constructing garments (e.g., sewing garment seams, waistbands, hems). The pathway of learning experiences was structured by engaging the apprentices in tasks of increasing accountability. This pathway included initially engaging the apprentices in tasks where mistakes could be tolerated (e.g., making children's garments and undergarments), and those where mistakes have significant consequences (e.g., ceremonial garments). The provision of indirect guidance through the apprentices' observation and listening made accessible and learnable the procedural knowledge required, as did the apprentices' participation in everyday work activities within these workshops. Hence, the workplaces' norms and practices provided a curriculum by structuring the apprentices' activities, thereby shaping their learning through experiences that were intentionally structured by pedagogical purposes.

Similar curriculum pathways of learning and their pedagogic properties have been identified elsewhere. In hairdressing salons, the tasks apprentices engage in and their progress through these hairdressing tasks are regulated by the particular salon's approach to hairdressing, including the preferences of the managers and owners, but also the demands of clientele (Billett, 2001). In one salon, where clients are attended to by a number of hairdressers, the apprentices first engage in 'tea and tidy' work that comprises providing hot beverages for clients and keeping the salon clean and tidy. These activities are not only important tasks, they are structured as necessary components in understanding and performing as a hairdresser. Through these activities, apprentices learn about and practice procedures for determining client needs, hygiene and maintaining cleanliness. For instance, identifying clients' needs and providing them with tea or coffee assist in building the apprentices' capacities and confidence to negotiate with clients. Next, apprentices engage in washing clients' hair and, after that, rinsing the chemicals used to shape and/or colour clients' hair. Participation in these tasks further develops the apprentices' capacities to communicate and negotiate with clients, and also to learn more demanding techniques. Throughout, the apprentices learn inter-psychologically through direct interpersonal interactions with experienced hairdressers and more indirectly through observation and listening that helps them to understand and practice the important components of each task (e.g., the importance of removing all the chemicals), and each task's place in and significance to the hairdressing process. Later, apprentices work with experienced hairdressers in placing rods and curlers in clients' hair. Then, before being permitted to cut women's hair, they commence cutting men's hair, which is held to be less difficult and of lower error likelihood than addressing women's hair. The apprentices continue on this path of activities and engagement in practice until they can independently style hair. In this way, the hairdressing apprentices progress along a track that incrementally and sequentially provides them with more demanding tasks (i.e., new learning), and ensures practice (i.e., refinement) of those tasks that assist in the development of the apprentices' workplace practice. This track of activities constitutes a central principle of a workplace curriculum, and one founded on maintaining the workplace's viability. This principle may prove to be broadly applicable across different kinds of work.

However, within the same occupation workplace requirements are not uniform; therefore the curriculum pathways may be quite particular to each workplace. This lack of uniformity likely means that there is a distinct set of rules for the division of labour in each salon, which may apply to other kinds of workplaces. In one salon the task of hairdressing was very widely distributed across the staff in the salon, with the most senior hairdresser completing the haircut which may well have been started by one hairdresser, taken over by another, and then passed on to a third or fourth hairdresser. Yet in another salon the same hairdresser undertakes the entire hairdressing task. In this latter salon the apprentice is required to learn to cut and colour independently far earlier than in the first salon. The structuring of activities in the second salon includes gaining competence with procedures that permit early independent practice (ibid.). Therefore, in the same occupation of practice, the particular workplace's goals and practices will shape the structuring and sequencing of the activities that constitute the kinds of tasks to be undertaken and to what standard: the intended workplace curriculum. These two salons, like the others in the study, have distinct hairdressing goals and practices, and different bases for their continuity. These distinct imperatives are reinforced by the localised factors that together constitute a particular workplace curriculum. It follows, therefore, that there is a need to acknowledge and understand localised requirements, and this is well recognised within curriculum practices for educational settings. For instance, Skilbeck's (1984) study of school-based curriculum emphasises the importance of accounting for and accommodating local factors in organizing the goals and experiences for students' learning. However, one important consideration here is that the requirements for work and what constitutes expertise (i.e., being able to resolve non-routine problems) are likely to be situationally ordered (Billett, 2001). That is, there is no such thing as a vocational expert per se, but rather the particular situational requirements suggest that localised factors will likely always constitute what comprises expert performance. It is postulated from the study above that hairdressers from one or other salon would not simply be able to move to the other salon and practice competently, in the short term, until they had acquired the particular capacities for performance in localised requirements. For instance, beyond the differences in the kinds of hairdressing techniques required across these salons, there were also particular capacities that needed to be developed. For instance, in one salon performing as a hairdresser required being able to manage difficult and argumentative clients, and in the absence of the salon's owner. In another, a key performance requirement was to know the personal histories of clients and to be able to engage with them in conversations about events in their lives. Rather than knowledge of the clients' personal history and affiliations being a peripheral capacity, many of the clients in this salon came for companionship and social interaction, as much as having the haircut.

Consequently, and ultimately, organising and enacting a learning curriculum is something that needs to be done at the local level. While it may be possible to identify broadly the kinds of experiences that need to be sequenced in order for a novice, for instance, to move through to practice an occupation, the actual conduct of that occupation requires competence within a particular instance of that practice because the organisation of work, its goals and purposes, and its means of enactment, are situationally distinct (ibid.). All of this suggests that the organisation of the learning curriculum and its enactment cannot best progress remotely from the practice it addresses.

Enacting the learning curriculum

This section seeks to set out some bases for organising and enacting the learning curriculum as it might be applied to particular workplace settings of different kinds. It proposes that the organisation and enactment of a learning curriculum has at least three dimensions: i) structuring the pathway of activities; ii) identifying learning that requires the assistance of others or particular experiences (e.g., hard-to-learn knowledge); and iii) identifying and utilising pedagogically rich activities. The first dimension refers to identifying the type and ordering of the experiences for the learners as they participate in the workplace activities and move on to engage in more demanding and complex tasks. The second refers to identifying activities and tasks which are unlikely to be learned through discovery alone, and, therefore, require the assistance of more experienced co-workers to secure or make the learning of those tasks attainable for the learners, through direct guidance. The third dimension refers to identifying and engaging learners in activities within the workplace that have particularly powerful pedagogic properties, and from which novices can richly learn.

Structuring a pathway of activities

As suggested above, in many workplaces it is not necessary to organise the overall structure of the learning curriculum, because it already exists. That is, there is often an understanding in workplaces about the sequencing of activities in which workers engage that is commensurate with their level of competence. Hence, the norms and practices associated with participating in the workplace are quite likely to be already understood and enacted. Nevertheless, it can be worthwhile to map out this pathway so that it is explicit and clearly understood, and also seek to make its progression more structured. Also, the organisation of these experiences is sometimes informed by others (e.g., managers, employers), rather than those who may best understand that sequence (i.e., those who undertake the work). Hence, it is useful to identify the sequence that people who work in the area believe novices should follow when learning about the work activity and its practices. For instance, against what appeared to be a logical process of moving from product to outcome (as I had done all those years ago), in one food processing company the workers are taught that to learn the required tasks for that workplace it is best to start out working in the packaging and storage area in order to understand what happens to the products once they have been manufactured (Billett & Boud, 2001). The production workers felt that it was important to understand how the products needed to be organised in uniformly weighted packs that would fit in cardboard containers, which in turn would fit with others in boxes of such containers, and then be stored in pallets in preparation for their delivery to shops and supermarkets. Thus, starting in the warehouse was proposed to be the best way in which the learning curriculum for workers in this area should progress. It was suggested that the novice would then move through the production process in almost the reverse order of the flow of production in order to understand how central the mixing of products and the manufacturing process which occurred early in the production cycle were to the processes that followed it. Hence, an explicit understanding of these requirements would be central to understanding the performance require-ments in the mixing and preparation of the food products.

Identifying the learning curriculum can be approached in two quite different ways. First, individuals can be asked to indicate a listing and sequencing of tasks that need to be learnt. To generate a comprehensive list of tasks or activities and a sequencing of those activities, a lined sheet of paper and prompts about con-sidering which tasks need to be performed daily, weekly and less frequently, as well as those that may never need to be performed yet are required to be learnt (e.g., emergency or safety procedures) can be used. In this approach, the infor-mants generate a list of tasks and indicate the sequence for novices engaging in and learning about these tasks. The second approach is to secure from the work-place some statement about the kind of tasks workers are expected to do, from a job specification sheet or work profile for instance. This approach is used to provide a more complete set of prompts to help the informants account for all of the activities that need to be sequenced for their learning. The informants are asked to reflect upon the list and either add or delete any that need to be included or are seen to be unnecessary. As with the first approach, the informants are asked to indicate the sequence in which these tasks should be undertaken, and, hence, learnt. Consequently, whichever way is used, the process generates a list of sequenced activities that comprise the basis for the learning curriculum for that workplace or specific occupational practice.

Curiously, when undertaking this process in workplaces there has been, to date, high levels of consensus from both expert and novice informants about the sequencing of activities to be learnt. However, should there be any discrepancy, it might be sensible to privilege the views of those who actually conduct the work not those who have opinions about how the work should be conducted. That is, those who actually perform the work may well have insights and understandings which are informed through actual practice. Of course, this approach is likely to be generative of what is currently occurring rather than what others would like to see occur. Through these processes, however, the ordering of a set of experiences can be identified and set out as a pathway of experiences: a curriculum. It could be that some bases for improving that sequence might be identified through a careful consideration of what informants propose. One final consideration is that not all individuals learning in the workplace are moving along novice to expert trajectories. Much of the curriculum literature assumes this is the case, as do many of the models of curriculum development and progression. However, in workplaces individuals can also be engaged in extending their skills into new areas, albeit with a strong base of existing knowledge about the workplace, even the work area and, possibly, much observed knowledge about the work area they are learning more about. Hence, the sequence and trajectory of the learning curriculum needs also to be open to the prospect of different kinds of 'courses to run', and these may be quite distinct from those taken by novices.

Identifying hard-to-learn knowledge

Although much of what needs to be learnt through workplace experiences can be learnt through workers' engagement in everyday activity, as is suggested in the anthropological literature, this will not always be the case. That is, there is much, and perhaps an increasing amount of, knowledge that will not be learnt through discovery learning alone. In particular, the increased incidence of tasks that are premised on understanding symbolic or conceptual knowledge are of the kind that will not be learnt through observing and listening to others and then attempting to practice through a process of imitation and modelling. Instead, these tasks may well require the intervention of a more experienced other, and even the use of particular learning strategies to assist that learning. For instance, it has been noted that an increasing component of the knowledge required for work is opaque and hard to learn. In particular, contemporary technology often makes the process of understanding the requirements to work more difficult because those requirements are not so easy to experience and understand (Zuboff, 1988). The symbolic conceptual knowledge required to operate a computer-controlled lathe is quite different from the tacit procedural and conceptual knowledge required for a manual lathe (Martin & Scribner, 1991). Hence, there is likely to be a need to identify this kind of knowledge and also consider how best it might be learnt through practice-based experiences. Consequently, as well as getting workers to sequence the activities that need to be learnt, it may well be very helpful for them to indicate how easy these tasks are to learn.

The aim here is to identify those tasks that may require assistance to learn. Indications of difficulty to learn can be obtained by getting informants to allocate a grading system to a particular task (e.g., no star or one star for tasks that are easy to learn, five stars for a task which is very difficult to learn). This exercise can be done on the task listing referred to above. However, unlike the consensus on what constitutes the sequencing of activities required to be learnt, it is likely that there will be significant differences in accounts of what is easy and difficult to learn between experienced and novice practitioners. The accounts that will be most credible will come from those who have recently learned those tasks. Experts who have long since learned the tasks and can perform them quite easily may not recall or even understand how difficult some of the tasks are to learn. Moreover, through practice, they will have come to proceduralise many of their skills which render them difficult to recall or even articulate.

Consequently, my advice is to accept the word of the relative novices who have recently learned the tasks as their accounts are likely to be more valid than those of the experts who have long since learnt the tasks and may have forgotten how demanding they were to learn. In this way it is possible to identify the particular activities which will need the support of a more experienced or expert counterpart, and possibly need greater access to close guidance by that expert, which might extend to the use of specific guided learning strategies. These could include the use of modelling, coaching and scaffolding for developing procedural capacities, and strategies such as questioning, the use of analogies, diagrams and explanations to develop conceptual capacities.

Yet, there are also other reasons for identifying particular kinds of activities, including those activities that inherently provide opportunities for rich learning.

Identifying and utilising pedagogically rich activities

Some activities are inherently predisposed to providing rich learning experiences. Consequently, it is worth identifying those activities and finding ways of encouraging novices or more experienced workers to access and engage quite deliberately in those experiences. For instance, within nursing it has been long recognised that a particularly rich pedagogic activity is the 'handover' which occurs at the end and beginning of each nursing shift on hospital wards. As the incoming shifts of nurses arrive they are briefed by the nurses who are just completing their shift in order to hand over the care of the patients. The process typically appears to engage the nurses in a discussion about: i) the patients; ii) their condition(s); iii) the treatments they are receiving; iv) how they are responding to those treatments; and v) what the prognosis is for their progression. This activity then provides the opportunity to develop understandings, linkages, modelling of processes and an increasingly wider set of understandings and linkages between patients' conditions, treatments and outcomes. Moreover, this activity can be engaged in by individuals with different levels of knowledge because it can provide rich learning experiences of different kinds. For instance, a novice student nurse can come to relate the language, concepts and use of terminology that they have experienced in the educational setting to what they are encountering in the hospital setting. A more experienced student will be able to make links between the patient's condition and the treatment they are having, and become aware of the links and associations. A final year nurse or experienced nurse will likely engage in the discussion which includes weighing up different approaches to patient care and deliberating upon how the particular patient is responding to their treatment or care, and what the likely outcome is for them.

The opportunity to discuss and debate the merits of different approaches and the likely outcomes with more experienced nurses clearly stands as an active and engaged learning process which is mediated by the access to other nurses and experts. These activities position the participants in active processes of comparing and contrasting, monitoring and projecting, analysing and arriving at conclusions about the patient's progress, and the merits of different approaches. All of these qualities make handovers particularly rich learning experiences, something that has long been recognised by nurses. Therefore, it is often standard practice that students and junior nurses participate in these handovers because they comprise potentially rich learning experiences. This is more likely to be the case if the learner is actively engaged and participating in the process of considering and making decisions across the five key focuses of the handovers. There are also other examples of opportunities to engage in rich learning experiences, such as the hospital ward rounds and when particular experiences occur in hospital wards (e.g., cardiac arrests). Other kinds of activities might include planning processes, such as teachers coming together to plan a process of instruction, or the organisation of a unit of coursework. In addition, some workplaces make specific efforts to involve novices or even experienced workers in processes they have not had the opportunity to engage in previously in order to extend the scope of the competence through learning about that process. Indeed, this process is apparently a key feature of learning through workplaces in large Japanese corporations (Dore & Sako, 1989). Consequently, these teachable moments need to be identified and utilised in assisting learners to develop the kind of knowledge that they need for effective practice. Part of this utilisation is preparing learners to identify and engage in such experiences in order to learn effectively. The educational worth of these experiences may not always be explicit or easy to understand (is not the handover merely a meeting of nurses?). Therefore, preparing learners to engage in and utilise those experiences is at least as important as providing those experiences. Moreover, arrangements should be made for identifying these experiences and permitting access for novices or learners.

The learning curriculum in prospect

In this chapter, a rationale for some bases and prospects for a workplace learning curriculum has been advanced and elaborated on. The discussion here may well contribute to broadening the debate about curriculum more generally, being something that is largely situated within, and a product of, experiences in educational institutions. Indeed, the idea of a personal curriculum that was mooted early in this chapter indicates something of the prospect for a broader view of curriculum that shifts the focus away from what is intended and enacted by social institutions such as schools, colleges and universities. However, the focus in this chapter is the role that a learning curriculum can play in organising and enriching experiences in workplaces. Emphasised throughout is the idea that beyond the provision of experiences, their sequencing and enabling, there is a need for learners to engage in these experiences in ways that maximise their learning from them. Nevertheless, it is proposed that there are ways of sequencing and structuring experiences that are helpful in organising workers' learning through engagement in everyday practice in their workplaces. Clearly, given the emphasis on a pathway of experiences in workplaces, norms and practices that invite, structure, support and guide participation are likely to engage workers in the kinds of thinking, acting and learning that are important for effective vocational practice. Moreover, the degree of consonance between individuals' interests and what the workplace provides will be salient in shaping individuals' engagement in the kind of learning they desire, and in ways consistent with increasing the quality of their learning experience (Dewey, 1938).

Of course, workplaces are contested environments and access to experience and close guidance can never be assured and may even be denied for political or personal reasons. However, the same could be said about experiences provided in educational institutions. Nevertheless, what is suggested here is that these tentative bases for a workplace curriculum are founded in empirical work and are consistent with many curriculum concepts and practices used in educational institutions and practices. Also proposed here is a way of understanding how the processes of engaging in and learning through socially situated practices, such as those in workplaces, educational institutions, community organisations and even families, which aim to secure the continuity of that practice, are shaped and complicated by circumstances in which different interests and power relationships are embedded and enacted. Individuals will likely interpret and construe meaning in ways that are consistent with their own personal goals and trajectories (Valsiner, 2000). So the deliberations here comprise a base from which to consider curriculum and pedagogic practices across the diverse social settings that constitute contemporary workplaces, where individuals participate in work and engage in learning throughout their working lives. The intention here is to advise others about these practices and for those others to then consider and appraise their utility for the promotion of occupational learning in which they are interested and engaged. Furthermore, the kinds of deliberations here about social practice, workplaces and individuals' personal curriculum might well assist in extending the concept of curriculum beyond the constraints of its conceptualisation being privileged by what occurs in educational institutions. They may also assist in understanding how the organisation of learning might be conceptualised for other kinds of social practice, albeit in the community, organisations, homes or other settings where social practices and individuals interact. In all, the discussion emphasises how social practices afford experiences in which to participate and learn. Yet it also highlights that, beyond the provision of activities and interactions extended by the social practices, individuals, within reasonable constraints, will choose how they participate and learn. That is, the participatory practices that constitute curriculum in a range of social settings comprise a negotiation between the continuities of both individuals and social practices.

Continuing the case study, and reflections upon it

To conclude, and returning to the case that opened this chapter, some noteworthy points include the fact that although experiences in workplace settings are held by some to develop only very specific forms of knowledge which are limited to the circumstances of their acquisition, this was not my experience. Indeed, the knowledge I learnt through that experience provided the foundation that I subsequently adapted throughout a career in clothing manufacturing, and also through a period of time as a costume maker for theatre, and then back to manufacturing, and then on to being a vocational teacher of clothing design and construction. Hence, rather than being concrete and specific, and limited in their adaptability, these experiences developed highly transferable or adaptable forms of knowledge at both the specific skill level (e.g., how to operate sewing machines and perform a range of procedures) and the highly strategic skills associated with the organisation of the manufacture of garments to specified standards, and in addressing a range of variables.

The process of learning I experienced was one characterised by engagement in a range of activities; by the opportunity to practice participating with other workers in being able to see how the tasks I was engaged with related to other tasks; by having the opportunity for repeated practice to develop strong procedural capacities, to understand critical performance requirements and some opportunity to see how these requirements varied from situation to situation; and by gaining an understanding of the particular set of sequences that are necessary for the effective production of garments. There were clear intentions for the organisation of these experiences by my employer that were richly pedagogic, had lasting consequences for my learning and contributed significantly to my personal curriculum. Hence, many years ago I came to realise that the experiences within practice settings were very important for my learning in order for me to become a competent occupational practitioner. However, a caveat is necessary here. The emphasis on the qualities and contributions of learning through practice settings is not meant to indicate that the college component of my preparation was irrelevant to my capacity to be effective in my work. That is far from the case; on many occasions throughout my career the knowledge I learnt in my course proved to be invaluable. The problem was that the transfer of what I had learnt in college was strongly inhibited by the fact that all of my experiences initially were in the college, and it was far from apparent how these experiences were aligned with those in the workplaces which employed me. My exposure to workplaces was very limited, and the application of the knowledge I was learning in college to particular workplaces was largely unknown to me, as were the ways and requirements of different workplaces, and the diverse nature of clothing manufacture across different workplaces.

Curiously, many years later when training to become a novice vocational educator I experienced an organised structuring of experiences that assisted me in becoming a teacher, and which combined my two sets of experiences more effectively. I was employed in a vocational education system which sponsored my development because of my relevant industry experience and knowledge. The course began with a two-week programme on preparing for teaching in a classroom situation (e.g., lesson planning, instructional methods, student assessment, understanding student backgrounds, etc.), followed by a semester of teaching in my host vocational college albeit on a light timetable. I had my own classes and had to take full responsibility for planning students' experiences, enacting those experiences and assessing students. My teaching activities were supported by an experienced and competent teacher education coordinator, who provided assistance, observed and gave feedback on my lessons and supported me on my journey to becoming a vocational educator. In the following semester, I attended a teaching college and completed courses associated with teacher education. In the semester after that one, I was back at my vocational college teaching students with a heavier timetable, and then the final semester was spent back at the teacher's college to complete my preparation and secure a teaching diploma. Yet, perhaps unlike the experiences of many students in teacher education courses, the programme in which I was engaged was an in-service rather than a pre-service programme. Hence, the lecturers at the teaching college did not necessarily have the experience or the expertise that the students had, which led to a more informed and sometimes quite argumentative interrelationship between the teaching college staff and the cohort of these 'in-service' students. Our experience of the overall curriculum, including what the teaching college lecturers provided, was perhaps quite different to that of those students who did not have the experience of teaching in schools until the third year of their four-year degree programme. Hence, the enactment of the curriculum and our experience of it was likely based on quite different premises than for those students whose experiences were formed overwhelmingly in the teacher's college. The point here is that we were engaging in a set of experiences which crossed both the educational institution and the workplace settings in which we taught and that ultimately comprised a personal curriculum. The uniqueness of this personal curriculum was shaped by previous histories, differences in the kinds of experiences we encountered in our host colleges, the demands of occupational preparation and the cultural practice of teaching across different occupations that was far from consistent. Hence, in addition to the practices of the workplace manifesting themselves as the learning curriculum there is a need to consider the concept of a personal curriculum as well.

References

Australian Industry Group (2007). *Skilling the existing workforce*. Canberra: Australian Industry Group.

Bailey, T. R., Hughes, K. L., & Moore, D. T. (2004). *Working knowledge: Work-based learning and educational reform*. New York: RoutledgeFalmer.

Bennett, C. A. (1938). 'The ancestry of vocational education', in E. A. Lee (ed.), *Objectives and problems of vocational education* (pp. 1–19). New York: McGraw-Hill Book Company.

Billett, S. (1993). 'Authenticity and a culture of workpractice', *Australian and New Zealand Journal of Vocational Education Research*, 2(1), 1–29.

Billett, S. (2001). *Learning in the workplace: Strategies for effective practice*. Sydney: Allen and Unwin.

Billett, S. (2006). *Informing post-school pathways through co-opting school students' authentic work experiences*. Adelaide: National Centre of Vocational Education Research.

Billett, S. (2009a). 'Personal epistemologies, work and learning', *Educational Research Review*, 4, 210–219.

Billett, S. (2009b). 'Realising the educational worth of integrating work experiences in higher education', *Studies in Higher Education*, 34(7), 827–843.

Billett, S. (2010). 'The practices of learning through occupations', in S. Billet (ed.), *Learning through practice: Models, traditions, orientations and approaches* (pp. 59–81). Dordrecht, The Netherlands: Springer.

Billett, S., & Boud, D. (2001). 'Participation in and guided engagement at work: Workplace pedagogic practices'. Paper presented at the 2nd International Conference on Learning and Work, Calgary.

Bloomer, M., & Hodkinson, P. (2000). 'Learning careers: Continuity and change in young people's dispositions to learning', *British Education Research Journal*, 26(5), 583–598.

Brown, J. S., Collins, A., & Duguid, P. (1989). 'Situated cognition and the culture of learning', *Educational Researcher*, 18(1), 32–34.

Cho, M. K., & Apple, M. (1998). 'Schooling, work and subjectivity', *British Journal of Sociology of Education*, 19(3), 269–291.

Collins, A., Brown, J. S., & Newman, S. E. (1989). 'Cognitive apprenticeship: Teaching the crafts of reading, writing and mathematics', in L. B. Resnick (ed.), *Knowing, learning and instruction: Essays in honour of Robert Glaser* (pp. 453–494). Hillsdale, NJ: Erlbaum & Associates.

Department of Innovation, Universities and Skills (2008). *Higher education at work*. London: Department of Innovation, Universities and Skills.

Dewey, J. (1938). *Experience and education*. New York: Macmillan.

Dore, R. P., & Sako, M. (1989). *How the Japanese learn to work*. London: Routledge.

Fuhrer, U. (1993). 'Behaviour settings analysis of situated learning: The case of newcomers', in S. Chaiklin & J. Lave (eds), *Understanding practice: Perspectives on activity and context* (pp. 179–211). Cambridge: Cambridge University Press.

Gott, S. (1989). 'Apprenticeship instruction for real-world tasks: The co-ordination of procedures, mental models, and strategies', *Review of Research in Education*, 15, 97–169.

Greeno, J. G. (1989). 'Situations, mental models, and generative knowledge', in D. Klahr & K. Kotovsky (eds), *Complex information processing: The impact of Herbert A. Simon*. Hillsdale, NJ: Erlbaum & Associates.

Greinhart, W.-D. (2002). *European and vocational training systems: The theoretical context of historical development. Towards a history of vocational education and training (VET) in Europe in a comparative perspective*. Florence: CEDEFOP: European Centre for the Development of Vocational Training.

Hodges, D. C. (1998). 'Participation as dis-identification with/in a community of practice', *Mind, Culture and Activity*, 5(4), 272–290.

Hodkinson, P., & Bloomer, M. (2002). 'Learning careers: Conceptualising lifelong work-based learning', in K. Evans, P. Hodkinson & L. Unwin (eds), *Working to learn: Transforming learning in the workplace* (pp. 29–43). London: Kogan Page.

Hodkinson, P. H., & Hodkinson, H. (2004). 'The significance of individuals' dispositions in the workplace learning: A case study of two teachers', *Journal of Education and Work*, 17(2), 167–182.

Hodkinson, P., Billett, S., & Bloomer, M. (2004). 'The significance of ontogeny and habitus in constructing theories of learning', *Studies in Continuing Education*, 26(1), 19–43.

Lave, J. (1990). 'The culture of acquisition and the practice of understanding', in J. W. Stigler, R. A. Shweder & G. Herdt (eds), *Cultural psychology* (pp. 259–286). Cambridge: Cambridge University Press.

Lodge, R. C. (1947). *Plato's theory of education*. London: Kegan Paul, Trench, Trubner.

Marsh, C., & Willis, G. (1995). *Curriculum: Alternative approaches, ongoing issues*. Englewood Cliffs, NJ: Merill.

Martin, L. M. W., & Scribner, S. (1991). 'Laboratory for cognitive studies of work: A case study of the intellectual implications of a new technology', *Teachers College Record*, 92(4), 582–602.

Palinscar, A. S., & Brown, A. L. (1984). 'Reciprocal teaching of comprehension-fostering and comprehension-monitoring activities', *Cognition and Instruction*, 1(2), 117–175.

Pelissier, C. (1991). 'The anthropology of teaching and learning', *Annual Review of Anthropology*, 20, 75–95.

Perkins, D., Jay, E., & Tishman, S. (1993). 'Beyond abilities: A dispositional theory of thinking', *Merrill-Palmer Quarterly*, 39(1), 1–21.

Quicke, J. (1999). *A curriculum for life: Schools for a democratic learning society*. Buckingham: Open University Press.

Raizen, S. A. (1991). *Learning and work: The research base. Vocational Education and Training for youth: Towards coherent policy and practice*. Paris: OECD.

Rogoff, B. (1990). *Apprenticeship in thinking – cognitive development in social context*. New York: Oxford University Press.

Rogoff, B., & Lave, J. (eds) (1984). *Everyday cognition: Its development in social context*. Cambridge, MA.: Harvard University Press.

Salomon, G. (1997). *Distributed cognitions: Psychological and educational considerations*. Cambridge: Cambridge University Press.

Scribner, S. (1985). 'Vygostky's use of history', in J. V. Wertsch (ed.), *Culture, communication and cognition: Vygotskian perspectives* (pp. 119–145). Cambridge: Cambridge University Press.

Sfard, A. (1998). 'On two metaphors for learning and the dangers of choosing just one', *Educational Researcher*, March, 4–13.

Skilbeck, M. (1984). *School based curriculum development*. London: Harper and Row.

Tobias, S. (1994). 'Interest, prior knowledge, and learning', *Review of Educational Research*, 64(1), 37–54.

Universities Australia (2008). *A national internship scheme: Enhancing the skills and work-readiness of Australian university graduates*. Canberra: Universities Australia.

Valsiner, J. (2000). *Culture and human development*. London: Sage Publications.

Wall, G. I. (1967/1968). 'The concept of vocational education', *Proceedings of the Philosophy of Education Society of Great Britain*, 2, 51–65.

Zuboff, S. (1988). *In the age of the smart machine: The future of work and power*. New York: Basic Books.

Chapter 3

Transformational learning: the perspective of J. Mezirow

Mien Segers and Maurice De Greef

Case study: the Mirror of Talents

The Mirror of Talents refers to an adult education programme using the telling and playing (theatre) of life stories as a social medium to connect elderly people and youngsters. On the one hand, it addresses the problem of the increasing social exclusion of elderly people, elderly people who increasingly do not participate in society due to feelings of detachment from the 'young' population. On the other hand, it deals with elderly people's feelings of fear, their perception of youngsters as 'different' and therefore 'offensive' in many ways. The main aim of the programme is to give seniors and youngsters the opportunity to develop an understanding of each other by constructive dialogue in which both viewpoints are reflected. It is expected that both target groups, by learning more about each other, will understand each other better and the contact between both groups will improve, enhancing the social inclusion of the seniors.

Because of differences in their backgrounds and upbringings, seniors and youngsters often have different norms and values. Both have different views on various aspects of life which can lead to misunderstandings and conflicts. Likewise, they also have different talents. It is precisely these talents that can establish the contact and bridge the gap between both generations.

A lot of seniors are very talented when it comes to telling stories about past days. When they tell the stories their eyes light up, they are energetic and they take plenty of time to explain in great detail how life was in the old days. A large number of them can also express this marvellously in their writings in which they tell their own life-story. These life-stories are used by the youths from a local theatre school as scripts. The youngsters play the life-stories of the elderly people. In this way, the enthusiasm of the youngsters for theatre and the enthusiasm of the seniors about their life-stories is combined. This results in a mix of the different viewpoints of both target groups. The seniors make their view of (their own) life explicit and the youths interpret this in their own way and translate it through their acting.

After a period of preparation (storytelling, story-writing by a professional, transforming stories into scripts by two theatre directors, practising the dramatisation of the play by the youngsters of the theatre school), during a three-hour event the youngsters play the life-stories of the seniors, with the seniors as their audience. After the play there are discussions among the youngsters and seniors and a closing debate showing both groups that age or generation did not matter; they shared the same needs and interests. Conservative youths and traditionalist seniors are sometimes diametrically opposed to progressive youths and liberal seniors. The added value of being so intensely involved with one another on this programme provides the opportunity to witness that someone from a different age group can offer a totally different view on life and can give the participants a renewed courage to take up life again, or simply gives the assurance that someone is just doing well. The three hours' theatre experience with discussions and debate results in people feeling reconnected to one another because they evidently do have so much in common. The seniors, by reflecting on their life experiences as expressed by the youngsters, are stimulated to choose other paths in their life, to participate more actively in a society they are connected to; this looking back at the past presents opportunities for the future (www.socialinclusion.eu).

Introduction

The Mirror of Talents case above describes an adult education programme aiming to contribute to the transformational learning of seniors as well as youngsters.

Transformational Learning (TL) or Transformative Learning was first articulated by Jack Mezirow in 1978 and since then this theory, following the Andragogy and Self-Directed Learning theory, has become very popular in the adult education area. This chapter gives an overview of Transformational or Transformative Learning theory, the critiques it receives and its application in practice.

In this chapter we focus mainly on Mezirow's point of view, but perspectives from other theorists are also included. First, we start with an introduction on TL by explaining three key concepts within the theory: experience; critical reflection; and development. Second, we explain Mezirow's theory in detail, including the key terms. The key terms include making meaning (interpretation), meaning schemes, meaning perspectives, critical reflection, perspective transformation, discourse and action (Mezirow, 1997, p. 60). Significant TL involves three phases: critical reflection on one's assumptions; discourse to validate the critically reflective insight; and action. The process of critical reflection, according to Mezirow, consists of several steps: a disorienting dilemma; a self-examination; a critical assessment of assumptions; recognising that others have gone through a similar process; exploring options for forming new roles; relationships or actions; formulating a plan of action; and reintegration back into one's life based on the new, transformed perspective (Mezirow, 1991).

Following the introduction of Mezirow's theory, we give an overview of recent research related to TL theory including critiques on Mezirow's theory and another perspective on TL theory by Robert Boyd. Critiques on Mezirow's theory mainly concern issues of social change, power relationships, context and rationality. Robert Boyd has developed a theory of transformational education that views TL as an 'intuitive, creative, emotional process' (Grabov, 1997, p. 90). After providing the introduction to Mezirow's theory and the critiques, we apply the theory to learning in the workplace and conclude this chapter with the elaboration of a case study.

The theory of Transformational Learning

Mezirow's Transformational Learning theory is about making meaning – how adults interpret their life experiences. He defines learning as a meaning-making activity: 'learning is understood as the process of using a prior interpretation to construe a new or a revised interpretation of the meaning of one's experience in order to guide future action' (Mezirow, 1996, p. 162). The term 'meaning making' (i.e., constructing meaning) is found most frequently in constructivist approaches, in which meaning is viewed as within ourselves and constructed from knowledge.

Mezirow (1990, p. 1) defines TL as 'the process of learning through critical self-reflection, which results in the reformulation of a meaning perspective to allow a more inclusive, discriminating, and integrative understanding of one's experience' and 'learning includes acting on these insights'. There are three key concepts (experience, critical reflection and development) that answer the questions of why to engage in TL, how to implement TL and what to achieve from TL. Mezirow (1995, p. 58) sees experience as the subject matter of transformative adult education. In childhood, unconsciously through socialisation, people learn many ways of understanding the world. These culturally determined perspectives usually remain unconscious in adulthood, but they are very important in determining the way we interpret experience (Mezirow, 1991). From childhood on, experience is socially constructed. However, experiences can be deconstructed, acted on and reconstructed (Michelson, 1996). To affect a transformation, experience itself is not enough and critical reflection is necessary for the process. To reflect critically we must examine the underlying beliefs and assumptions that affect how we make sense of the experience. The entire process of TL is about change – change that is growth enhancing and developmental. Individual development is both inherent in and an outcome of the TL process. Several capacities of mind or consciousness are transformed through the processes of TL (Elias, 1997).

The process of TL consists of three phases: the first phase is critical reflection in which previous meaning perspectives are examined and reformulated and new perspectives are developed; the second phase is discourse in which the new perspectives are validated by consulting with well informed others; and the last phase is action in which people act, using the new perspectives, and the new perspectives are internalised and integrated with other perspectives.

Mezirow, architect of the theory of Transformational Learning

Jack Mezirow is the founder of the TL theory. Dr Jack Mezirow is Professor Emeritus of Adult and Continuing Education, Teachers College, Columbia University, Former Chairman, Department of Higher and Adult Education, and Director for Adult Education. His research interests are in the domains of adult learning and education. Well-known books are *Transformative dimensions of adult learning* (1991) and *Fostering critical reflection in adulthood* (& Associates, 1990). Moreover, he is the author of numerous other books, chapters, research reports and articles. Mezirow's TL theory is influenced by Freire's philosophy of education. He also draws ideas from the German philosopher Habermas.

Key terms

As TL theory has been evolving since its birth, terms used in this theory are diversely defined although the core idea remains the same. Among these key terms are making meaning, meaning schemes, meaning perspectives, reflection, critical reflection, perspective transformation and Transformational Learning. According to Mezirow (1990, 1991), these terms are defined as follows:

Transformational Learning 'the process of learning through critical self-reflection, which results in the reformulation of a meaning perspective to allow a more inclusive, discriminating, and integrative understanding of one's experience. Learning includes acting on these insights' (Mezirow, 1990, p. xvi).

Making meaning to make sense of an experience, that is, make an interpretation of it. Interpretation involves making a decision that may result in confirmation, rejection, extension or formulation of a belief or meaning scheme, or in finding that that belief or scheme presents a problem that requires further examination. When we subsequently use this interpretation to guide decision-making or action, then making meaning becomes learning.

Meaning schemes specific beliefs, feelings, attitudes, emotional reactions and value judgments articulated by an interpretation; they are sets of related and habitual expectations governing if-then, cause-effect and category relationships as well as event sequences; they are derived from earlier, often unreflective interpretations. The meaning schemes that make up meaning structures may change as an individual adds to or integrates ideas within an existing scheme and, in fact, this transformation of meaning schemes occurs routinely through learning (adapted from Imel, 1998).

Meaning perspectives groups of related meaning schemes; they are the structures of assumptions that constitute a frame of reference for interpreting the meaning of an experience; they are broad, generalised, orienting predispositions;

they are the lens through which each person filters, engages and interprets the world; they involve the application of habits or expectations to objects or events to form an interpretation. Meaning perspectives are, for the most part, uncritically acquired in childhood through the process of socialisation. These meaning structures are frames of reference that are based on the totality of the individuals' cultural and contextual experiences and influence how they behave and interpret events (adapted from ibid.).

Reflection   'the examination of the justification for one's beliefs, primarily to guide action and to reassess the efficacy of the strategies and procedures used in problem solving' (Mezirow, 1990, p. xvi).

Critical reflection   the assessment of the validity of the presuppositions of one's meaning perspectives, and the examination of their sources and consequences.

Meaning perspective transformation   the process of becoming critically aware of how and why our presuppositions have come to constrain the way we perceive, understand and feel about our world; of reformulating these assumptions to permit a more inclusive, discriminating, permeable and integrative perspective; and of making decisions or otherwise acting on these new understandings.

Key elements

TL posits experience as its starting point and as its content for reflection. Engaging the life experience in a critically reflective manner is a necessary condition for transformation. The entire process is about change – change that is growth enhancing and developmental. Experience, critical reflection and development are three key elements of TL. The elaboration of these concepts includes other theorists' ideas as well as Mezirow's.

Experience   one of the assumptions of andragogy is that adults bring with them a depth and breadth of experience that can be used as a resource for their and others' learning (Knowles, 1980). As the subject matter of TL, experiences differ and some of them are more useful than others. Experience is seen as socially constructed rather than as unmediated (Michelson, 1996). Therefore, it can be deconstructed, acted on, and reconstructed. According to Tennant (1991, p. 197), 'the meanings that learners attach to their experiences may be subjected to critical scrutiny'. To facilitate adult learning, the teachers may consciously try to disrupt the learner's world view and stimulate uncertainty, ambiguity and doubt in learners about previously taken-for-granted interpretations of experience. Jarvis (1992, p. 15) explains how experience stimulates learning:

> While all learning begins with experience, this is not experience for which the learners already have a solution or response. Adults with all their memories

of previous experiences and their store of knowledge, are unable to respond (to the new experience) . . . There is a disjuncture at a particular point in time between people's biographies – that is, their internalized cultural patterns of social living – and their experience.

It is 'at this point of disjuncture' that 'individuals are forced to ask why this has occurred to them or what it means' (ibid.). These questions are located at the start and at the core of human learning.

Critical reflection   with an experience that one cannot accommodate into the prior life structure, the transformative learning process can begin. Necessary to the process is critical reflection. Experience itself is not enough to lead to transformation. What is valuable is the intellectual growth that follows the process of reflecting on experience. To reflect critically, we must examine the underlying beliefs and assumptions that affect how we make sense of the experience. Mezirow (1991) differentiates three types of reflection, of which only one can lead to transformative learning. Content reflection is thinking about the actual experience itself. Process reflection is thinking about ways to deal with the experience, that is, problem-solving strategies. Premise reflection involves examining long-held, socially constructed assumptions, beliefs and values about the experience or problem. Only premise reflection can contribute to TL. The steps of critical reflection will be explained in the following section on the phases of TL.

Both Taylor (1994), who studied adults who had lived and worked in another country, and McDonald (1997), who investigated how people became ethical vegans, found some people who had transformed their perspective without being aware of the change process. This fact raises questions about the necessity of critical reflection for a transformation to take place. Mezirow (1998, p. 191) has suggested that transformations may occur through the process of assimilative learning. By this he means that 'our situation changes, and, beyond our scope of awareness, we make a tacit judgment to move toward a way of thinking or behaving that we deem more appropriate to our new situation.' Mezirow concedes that 'dramatic changes in orientation based upon assimilation rather than critical reflection on assumptions' are possible.

Development   individual development is both inherent in and an outcome of the TL process. The ability to think critically, which is necessary in order to result in a transformation, is itself developmental; that is, we can become better, more critical thinkers. Several capacities of mind or consciousness are transformed through the processes of TL (Elias, 1997): development of a 'conscious I' capable of exercising critical reflection; the development of the capacity for transformational thinking to be more dialectical or systemic; and the development of the capacity to be a conscious creative force in the world. King and Kitchener's reflective judgment model consists of seven stages, of which only the last two are characteristic of critical reflection: 'knowledge is not a "given" but must be actively constructed and claims of knowledge must be understood in relation to the context in which they are generated' (King & Kitchener, 1994, p. 66).

Mezirow (1998, p. 189) notes that a person moves through developmental stages: 'It seems clear that movement through these ways of knowing, related to age and education, is toward a more inclusive, differentiating, permeable, critically reflective, and integrative frame of reference.' Development is also the outcome of transformative learning. Mezirow (1991, p. 155) states clearly that the process of perspective transformation is 'the central process of adult development', 'meaning perspectives that permit us to deal with a broader range of experience, to be more discriminating, to be more open to other perspectives, and to better integrate our experiences are superior perspectives' (Mezirow, 1990, p. 14). 'Transformative learning involves becoming more reflective and critical, being more open to the perspectives of others and being less defensive against and more accepting of new ideas' (Booth & Segon, 2009, p. 22).

Phases of Transformational Learning

According to Mezirow (1997, p. 60), significant TL involves three phases: 'critical reflection on one's assumptions, discourse to validate the critically reflective insight, and action'.

The first phase of TL – *the critical reflection process* – includes ten steps:

- disorienting dilemmas
- self-examination
- critical assessment of assumptions
- recognition that others have shared similar transformations
- exploration of new roles or actions
- development of a plan of action
- acquisition of knowledge and skills for implementing the plan
- trying out the plan
- development of competence and self-confidence in new roles, and
- reintegration into life on the basis of new perspectives.

The step to develop a plan of action involves four steps within itself:

- acquiring knowledge and skills for implementing the plan
- trying out new roles
- negotiating new relationships or renegotiating existing relationships, and
- building competence and self-confidence in new roles.

Disorienting dilemmas function as catalysts for transformative learning. These dilemmas prompt critical reflection and the development of new ways of interpreting experiences when they do not fit in the previous experiences and problem-solving strategies. In this way, transformative learning involves:

becoming critically aware of how and why our assumptions have come to constrain the way we perceive, understand, and feel about our world; changing these structures of habitual expectation to make possible a more inclusive, discriminating, and integrating perspective; and, finally, making choices or otherwise acting upon these new understandings.

(Mezirow, 1991, p. 167)

Garrison (1991) also produces a theory of critical thinking that consists of five stages:

- identifying the problem
- defining the problem
- exploring ways of dealing with it
- applying one of the strategies to the problem, and
- finally integrating the new perspective.

He maintains that this process is congruent with Mezirow's perspective transformation. Brookfield's (1987, 1994) model of critical thinking includes five steps:

- trigger event
- appraisal
- exploration
- developing alternative perspectives, and
- integration.

Brookfield's model is identical to the ten-step process of transformative learning suggested by Mezirow. In his formulation of critical reflection, Brookfield echoes a more radical political stance.

The second phase of TL is *discourse*. To test whether our new meanings are true and authentic, Mezirow (1995, p. 53) says we must 'seek the best judgment of the most informed, objective, and rational persons we can find' and enter into 'a special form of dialogue'. Drawing from the German philosopher, Jürgen Habermas, this special form of dialogue is called 'discourse':

Discourse involves an effort to set aside bias, prejudice, and personal concerns and to do our best to be open and objective in presenting and assessing reasons and reviewing the evidence and arguments for and against the problematic assertion to arrive at a consensus.

(Ibid., p. 54)

The 'ideal' conditions for discourse are: having complete information; being free from self-deception; being able to evaluate arguments objectively; having an 'equal opportunity to participate in the various roles of discourse' and so on (ibid.).

Dialogue and discourse can proceed in a critically self-reflective manner that aims toward more sensitive, respectful, non-dominating, and non-distorting communication. Facilitating this kind of learning which views difference as an opportunity, a challenge to our abilities to communicate, understand, and learn, is precisely what adult education is about.

(Ibid., p. 55)

Discourse is not a war or a debate; it is a conscientious effort to find agreement, to build a new understanding.

(Mezirow, 1996, p. 170)

The third phase of TL is *action*. The type of action one takes 'depends upon the nature of the disorienting dilemma' (Mezirow, 1997, p. 60) and can range from making a decision to radical political protest. For critics who see the goal of adult education as social action, Mezirow's theory, with its emphasis on individual transformation, is too egocentric (Taylor, 1997).

Critiques and related research on Mezirow's Transformational Learning

A number of critical responses to Mezirow's theory of TL have emerged over the years (Taylor, 1998). We present the four most important critics.

One major area of contention surrounding Mezirow's theory is its emphasis on rationality. Boyd and Myers (1988) conclude that Mezirow grants rational critical reflection too much importance. They view transformative learning as an intuitive and emotional process. For Boyd (1989, p. 459), transformation is a 'fundamental change in one's personality involving the resolution of a personal dilemma and the expansion of consciousness resulting in greater personality integration'. First, an individual must be receptive or open to receiving 'alternative expressions of meaning', and then recognise that the message is authentic. Grieving, considered by Boyd to be the most critical phase of the discernment process, takes place when an individual realises that old patterns or ways of perceiving are no longer relevant, moves to adopt or establish new ways, and, finally, integrates old and new patterns. Unlike Mezirow, who sees the ego as playing a central role in the process of perspective transformation, Boyd and Myers (1988) use a framework that moves beyond the ego and the emphasis on reason and logic to a definition of transformative learning that is more psychosocial in nature. Rational thinking is a particularly Western concept, a product of the Enlightenment and Descartes' mind-body split. Even in the West, rationality is also gender specific, privileging men, those of the middle and upper classes, and whites (Merriam & Caffarella, 1999). Hanson (1996, p. 105) suggests that 'for some cultures and situations conformity to the group may be more important than critical autonomy. Self-reflection and critical thinking may be reputed to be universal "goods", but we need to be aware of their cultural specificity and power.'

The second critique concerning Mezirow's theory is 'the lack of a coherent, comprehensive theory of social change' (Collard & Law, 1989, p. 102). The main issue is that Mezirow emphasises the individual perspective transformation and fails to acknowledge the 'social environment in which structural inequalities are entrenched' (Collard & Law, 1989, p. 105). The social context is also of concern to Tennant (1993) who examines the developmental process inherent in transformative learning. He argues that 'what is, and what is not, more integration of experiences depends on the social and historical context in which experience occurs' (ibid., p. 38). He sees adult development as both social and psychological, and describes a person's life course as socially constructed. Larger societal and political changes will provoke critical reflection for some individuals (ibid.). The fall of communism, the elimination of the Berlin Wall, the escalation of violence against women – all such upheavals can lead an individual to question his or her values and beliefs. Good examples are the protests against the Iraq and the Vietnam Wars. Many people were led to reflect on values and assumptions related to democracy and communism, peace and war and the role of the United States in world politics. Many young adults seriously questioned their political views and philosophical beliefs, and rejected traditional views. Of course, social change does not necessarily lead to individual transformation; in fact Mezirow (1991) makes the opposite point that individual transformation leads to social action and social change. Changes can take place in both directions.

According to McDonald, Cervero and Courtenay (1999, p. 5) 'an enduring tension between Mezirow's transformation theory and its critiques is also the debate on the role of power in TL'. TL is optimised within ideal conditions of discourse, that is, communication free of distortions and manipulation, dominance-free forms of social relations. Hart (1985) sees power or dominance relationships as a barrier to adult learning. Power should be placed at the centre of transformative learning. For example, a person who becomes a vegetarian feels threatened, because friends and family laugh. Such action on the part of family and friends usually creates a painful dilemma for the developing vegetarian. Although these vegetarians were successful at changing their intrapersonal perspective, they never became completely free of the normative ideology of speciesism.

Finally, Clark and Wilson (1991) enter into the debate, presenting a critical response to Mezirow in which they argue that he fails to account for the cultural context of learning. Mezirow's theory appeared to be acontextual. His study looked at women returning to school, their experiences were studied as if they stood apart from their historical and sociocultural context, thereby limiting our understanding of the full meaning of those experiences. 'What he fails to do . . . is to maintain the essential link between the meaning of experience and the context in which it arises and by which it is interpreted' (ibid., p. 76). Mezirow agrees that his 1970s work does not include an analysis of social trends and that his original study was of white middle-class women returning to college. Additionally, Taylor's (1997) review of the empirical research on Mezirow's theory revealed a number of studies that found that aspects of the individual's biographical history and sociocultural factors shaped the nature of the transformative learning. Taylor points out that more attention given to such factors can help explain, for example, why a disorienting dilemma might lead to a perspective transformation for one person but not another.

Applications in the workplace

As workplace learning inevitably involves other people and common culture, TL is a relevant theory to help understand learning in the workplace. Sheila McCutchan (1997) was convincing in stating that human resource development strategies supported by transformative learning practice can support and sustain the development of a learning organisation. The key characteristic for the success of an organisation is its ability to learn. The traditional hierarchical management structures seem to be designed for controlling, rather than for learning. The fundamental challenge for organisations is to transform the capacities, to create knowledge; organisations must focus on how to create the conditions for learning. Building an organisation that can truly learn cannot be accomplished without developing a learning culture where people can learn and think. In such a culture, critical reflection can provide a foundation for dialogue which, when developed, can teach employees at all levels to go beyond their understanding of their assumptions and gain insight into a 'larger pool' of meaning for inquiry and feedback (Marsick & Watkins, 1994). Current organisational cultures may be unable to support the kind of learning needed to transform their capacity for learning and thinking (McCutchan, 1997). A culture is not easily changed. Organisations must first become aware of their cultural biases, and through reflection, dialogue and inquiry learn to become observers of their own thinking (Senge, 1990). Senge's description of transformative learning and the practice of critical reflection, by allowing for the potential transformation of personal frames of reference, lays the foundation for a new learning culture:

> The way companies are designed and managed, the way people's jobs are defined . . . the way we have been taught to think and interact . . . creates fundamental learning disabilities: status seeking behaviour, individualism, authoritarian, bureaucratic organisational structures, an 'us' versus 'them' mentality . . .
>
> (Ibid., p. 18)

In addition, there is the fear of something new, unpredictable or unknown; the uncomfortable realisation that in order to survive and thrive, individuals must change. However, for learning to occur, people must reach the psychological point where the fear of not learning is greater than the fear associated with entering the unknown (Schein, 1996). The individual differences among learners cannot be overlooked or neglected. The individual who is insecure or unsupported may not be able to overcome emotional barriers to learning and development (Cranton,

1994, p. 165). Society and the socialisation process 'militates against critical reflection' (Mezirow & Associates, 1990, p. 359). Barriers and learning disabilities abound within today's organisations and the transformation from hierarchical to democratic, from individualistic to team, from tunnel vision to systems thinking is a slow evolutionary process.

What is the educator's role? How can transformational learning be supported? The literature bombards educators with all of the things that they as educators are supposed to be: resource people, facilitators, counsellors, mentors, models, reformers and activists. Educators should love their subject, share the joys of studying, be knowledgeable, be good listeners, establish a supportive learning climate, use humour, provide positive feedback and so on (Brookfield, 1986). Now, with the emphasis in adult education on developing critical thinkers, facilitating self-directed learning, viewing self-directed learning as a political dimension of practice and fostering transformative learning, educators' roles grow even more complex (Cranton, 1994, p. 123). Also, since the educator is a model he should think critically about his teaching. In transformative learning it is important that the educator stimulates critical self-reflection. If the educator asks 'What are your underlying assumptions?' few people would be able to respond directly to the question. The educator can use strategies such as role-plays and simulations, writing critical incidents, completing a repertory grid, writing a life history, conducting a criteria analysis or engaging in a crisis-decision simulation. The three most important questions are 'What did you do?', 'How did you do it?' and 'Why did you do it?' The Mirror of Talents case study is a clear example of how in adult education programmes aiming to enhance the social inclusion of elderly people transformational learning can be scaffolded by using storytelling and theatre play.

Back to the case study

The Mirror of Talents is an adult education programme where making meaning is the core element. Storytelling and playing (theatre) serve as media to understand how a different age group perceives various aspects of life. The culturally determined meaning perspectives of both target groups (seniors and youngsters) are made conscious: the storytelling and playing makes clear how meaning perspectives determine the different ways of interpreting experience. The process of storytelling and story playing followed by debates is a process of meaning perspective transformation.

The Mirror of Talents illustrates the three key elements of transformational learning:

1   *Experience*: by storytelling, the seniors bring with them a depth and breadth of experience, used as a resource not only for their own learning and that of their peers, but also for that of the youngsters. The life experiences the seniors illustrate through their stories are very different and are socially constructed,

that is, constructed by the social environment in which they have participated. By storytelling, by observing the playing of their story as interpreted by the youngsters and finally through the debate, experiences are deconstructed, acted on and reconstructed. It leads to uncertainty, ambiguity and doubt in both the seniors and the youngsters about previously taken-for-granted interpretations of experience. It reflects the arguments of Jarvis (1992, p. 15) that 'at this point of disjuncture individuals are forced to ask why this has occurred to them or what it means. These questions are located at the start and at the core of human learning.'

2   *Critical reflection*: experience itself is not enough to lead to transformation. During the debate after the theatre play, critical reflection is the central process through which both seniors and youngsters examine the underlying beliefs and assumptions that affect how they make sense of the life experiences they have been telling and playing.

3   *Development*: the transformative learning of the Mirror of Talents programme involves becoming more reflective and critical, being more open to the perspectives of others, seniors as well as youngsters, and being less defensive against and more accepting of new ideas.

Referring to the three main phases in TL, the critical reflection process for the seniors starts with the storytelling, for the youngsters it starts with the story playing. For the seniors, it is the externalisation of how they experience and perceive the meaning of various life events. For the youngsters, by interpreting the seniors' stories in their theatre play, they critically reflect not only on the meaning perspectives of the seniors but also on theirs as reflected in the way they interpret the stories.

The debate after the theatre play refers to the second phase of transformational learning, the discourse. During the debate, differences in meaning perspectives are seen as an opportunity and a challenge to the seniors' as well as the youngsters' abilities to communicate, understand and learn (Mezirow, 1995).The third phase, action, is not part of the programme. The actions that the seniors as well as the youngsters take up after the Mirror of Talents programme can include a wide range of decisions with respect to social inclusion, from regularly walking in the city park to becoming politically active.

References

Booth, C., & Segon, M. (2009). 'A leadership and management development: An action research project', *International Review of Business Research Papers*, 5(4), 102–113.

Boyd, R. D. (1989). 'Facilitating personal transformations in small groups: Part I', *Small Group Behaviour*, 20(4), 459–474.

Boyd, R. D., & Myers, J. G. (1988). 'Transformative education', *International Journal of Lifelong Education*, 4, 261–284.

Brookfield, S. (1986). *Understanding and facilitating adult learning*. San Francisco, CA: Jossey-Bass.

Brookfield, S. (1987). *Developing critical thinkers*. San Francisco, CA: Jossey-Bass.

Brookfield, S. (1994). *Tales from the dark side: A phenomenography of adult critical reflection.* Proceedings of the Adult Education Research Conference. Knoxville: University of Tennessee.

Clark, M. C., & Wilson, A. L. (1991). 'Context and rationality in Mezirow's theory of Transformational Learning', *Adult Education Quarterly*, 41(2), 75–91.

Collard, S., & Law, M. (1989). 'The limits of perspective transformative: A critique of Mezirow's theory', *Adult Education Quarterly*, 39, 99–107.

Cranton, P. (1994). *Understanding and promoting transformative learning: A guide for educators of adults.* San Francisco, CA: Jossey-Bass.

Elias, Dean. (1997). 'It's time to change our minds: An introduction to transformative learning', *ReVision*, 20(1), 2–6.

Garrison, D. R. (1991). 'Critical thinking and adult education: A conceptual model for developing critical thinking in adult learners', *International Journal of Lifelong Learning*, 10(4), 287–303.

Grabov, V. (1997). 'The many facets of transformative learning theory and practice', in P. Cranton (ed.), *Transformative learning in action: Insights from practice* (pp. 89–96). San Francisco, CA: Jossey-Bass.

Hanson, A. (1996). 'The search for a separate theory of adult learning: Does anyone really need andragogy?', in R. Edwards, A. Hanson, & P. Raggatt (eds), *Boundaries of Adult Learning* (pp. 99–108). New York: Routledge.

Hart, M. (1985). 'Thematization of power, the search for common interests, and self-reflection: Towards a comprehensive concept of emancipatory education', *International Journal of Lifelong Education*, 4(2), 119–134.

Imel, S. (1998). *Transformative learning in adulthood.* Columbus, OH: ERIC Clearinghouse on Adult, Career and Vocational Education. Available at: http://www.ed.gov/databases/ERIC_Digests/ed423426.html.

Jarvis, P. (1992). *Paradoxes of learning: On becoming an individual in society.* San Francisco, CA: Jossey-Bass.

King, P. M., & Kitchener, K. S. (1994). *Developing reflective judgment.* San Francisco, CA: Jossey-Bass.

Knowles, M. S. (1980). *The modern practice of adult education: From pedagogy to andragogy.* New York: Cambridge Books.

McCutchan, S. (1997). 'Transformative Learning: Applications for the development of learning organisations'. Paper presented at the Midwest Research-to-Practice Conference in Adult, Continuing and Community Education, 15–17 October, Michigan State University.

McDonald, B. L. (1997). 'A comparison of Mezirow's Transformation Theory with the process of learning to become an ethical vegan'. Unpublished doctoral dissertation, University of Georgia.

McDonald, B., Cervero, R. M., & Courtenay, B. C. (1999). 'An ecological perspective of power in transformational learning: A case study of ethical vegans', *Adult Education Quarterly*, 50, 5–23.

Marsick, V., & Watkins, K. (1994). 'The learning organization: An integrative vision for HRD', *Human Resource Quarterly*, 5, 353–360.

Merriam, S. B., & Caffarella, R. S. (1999). *Learning in Adulthood.* San Francisco, CA: Jossey-Bass.

Mezirow, J. (1990). 'How critical reflection triggers transformative learning', in J. Mezirow & Associates, *Fostering critical reflection in adulthood: A guide to transformative and emancipatory learning* (pp. 1–20). San Francisco, CA: Jossey-Bass.

Mezirow, J. (1991). *Transformative dimensions of adult learning*. San Francisco, CA: Jossey-Bass.

Mezirow, J. (1995). 'Transformation theory of adult learning', in M. R. Welton (ed.), *Defense of the Lifeworld* (pp. 39–70). New York: State University of New York Press.

Mezirow, J. (1996). 'Contemporary paradigms of learning', *Adult Education Quarterly*, 46(3), 158–172.

Mezirow, J. (1997). 'Transformative theory out of context', *Adult Education Quarterly*, 48(1), 60–62.

Mezirow, J. (1998). 'On critical reflection', *Adult Education Quarterly*, 48(3), 185–198.

Mezirow, J., & Associates (1990). *Fostering critical reflection in adulthood: A guide to transformative and emancipatory learning*. San Francisco, CA: Jossey-Bass.

Michelson, E. (1996). 'Usual suspects: Experience, reflection and the (en)gendering of knowledge', *International Journal of Lifelong Education*, 15(6), 438–454.

Schein, E. (1996). 'Can learning cultures evolve?', *The Systems Thinker*, 7(6), 1–5.

Senge, P. (1990). *The Fifth Discipline*. New York: Doubleday.

Taylor, E. W. (1994). 'Intercultural competency: A transformative learning process', *Adult Education Quarterly*, 44(3), 154–174.

Taylor, E. W. (1997). 'Building upon the theoretical debate: A critical review of the empirical studies of Mezirow's Transformative Learning Theory', *Adult Education Quarterly*, 48(1), 34–59.

Taylor, E. W. (1998). 'The theory and practice of Transformative Learning: A critical review', Information Series No. 374. Columbus: ERIC Clearinghouse on Adult, Career, and Vocational Education, Center on Education and Training for Employment, College of Education, the Ohio State University.

Tennant, M. C. (1991). 'The psychology of adult teaching and learning', in J. M. Peters, P. Jarvis, & Associates (eds), *Adult education: Evolution and achievements in a developing field of study* (pp. 191–216). San Francisco, CA: Jossey-Bass.

Tennant, M. C. (1993). 'Perspective transformation and adult development', *Adult Education Quarterly*, 44(1), 34–42.

Chapter 4

The Experiential Learning Theory: D. Kolb and D. Boud

Mien Segers and Selma Van der Haar

Case study: A virtual simulation exercise of the Emergency Management Team

There is a fire in an electronics shop in the city centre. A bystander has called the fire brigade to say he has heard an explosion. It is noon; the owner and several customers were inside the building when the fire started. Moreover, next to the shop is a supermarket with many customers shopping at the time, and above the shop there are apartments for elderly people. The fire is growing.

This incident requires the coordinated help of the fire brigade, the police and disaster medicine. Each of these assistance units will send emergency staff as well as a Commander on Scene. These Commanders within the fire brigade, police and disaster medicine (the three assistance units) together form the Emergency Management Team. This implies it is a multidisciplinary team. It has the task of coordinating the cooperation of the different assistance units.

Since the kind of accidents in the electronics shop fortunately do not happen regularly, the Commanders on Scene of the three assistance units participate in training programmes based on virtual simulations to prepare them for these situations.

In the virtual simulations an incident and the assistance units are simulated. The burning shop and other buildings are visible on the computer screen, as well as the people on the street and the assistance units with their material. The virtual world is 'alive'. This means, for instance, that the people will move around when the technical support gives orders to do so, and the fire will expand depending on the reaction of the Commanders participating in the exercise. Each of the Commanders has his or her own computer screen and joystick and can walk through the virtual world. The Commanders will actually see each other as people in the virtual world. The assistance units are not present in person, but are played by a member of the training staff. These trainers provide information about the development of the incident and the effects of decisions. The Commanders initiate multidisciplinary meetings with each other to discuss what is actually happening and what should be done.

Making use of this virtual environment the Commanders practice their coordination and cooperation skills while pretending the incident is actually happening. They follow the procedures as in real time. Since the virtual world can be paused, process and progress can be evaluated any time.

The exercise design

The exercise starts with scenario 1 where the Commanders do their job: they explore the scene, develop an image of the situation and initialise and conduct a multidisciplinary meeting. After this first meeting the trainer takes a time-out and, together with the Commanders, evaluates the meeting. Together they reflect on what happened, what went well and what could be done better next time. Together they define what worked and what did not, and make a plan for what to do next time. Then the team starts scenario 2, and the members experiment with the plans and intentions developed. The same procedure is followed as in scenario 1. After one or two meetings the trainer stops the exercise and the meetings are evaluated again.

In these exercises central questions for the evaluation are:

- returning to the experience: what has happened and with what consequences?
- attending to feelings: what felt trustworthy and what felt inconvenient? What felt right and what felt wrong? What does this mean for the next meeting?
- re-examining in the light of the experience: what did this experience bring about in relation to the learning goals of the team? It can be helpful if the team members have written down learning goals when they start the exercise, so that they can reflect on their own notes.

Introduction

This chapter concerns the experiential learning paradigm, more precisely, the pivotal contributions of David Kolb and David Boud. Kolb's (1984) book *Experiential learning: Experience as the source of learning and development*, a pivotal work on experiential learning, was inspired by the ideas of many twentieth-century scholars, such as John Dewey, Kurt Lewin, Jean Piaget, Carl Jung and Carl Rogers. This book brings together the ideas of leading thinkers on experiential learning in explaining Kolb's theory. The six constituting propositions of the Experiential Learning paradigm are summarised in this chapter.

David Kolb is renowned in the educational field for his Learning Style Inventory (LSI), although it received more criticism than the Experiential Learning theory. The starting point of his model is the idea that learning preferences can be described using two continuums: active-reflective and abstract-concrete. This results in four types of learners:

- active-abstract (converger)
- active-concrete (accommodator)
- reflective-abstract (assimilator), and
- reflective-concrete (diverger).

The LSI is designed to determine an individual's learning preference (see http://en.wikipedia.org/wiki/David_A._Kolb).

David Boud's contribution focused on reflection as a key process in experiential learning. He defined reflective processes and elaborated on why reflection on action is necessary to learn from the experience. Considering experience as an interaction between the learner and the learning milieu, with continuous noticing and intervening becoming reflection in action, Boud explains that characteristics of both factors affect the success of the learning experience.

The final part of this chapter elaborates on the practical applications of the Experiential Learning paradigm in the workplace. The case study will be revisited from an experiential learning perspective.

Kolb, the architect of experiential learning

David Kolb is a professor of organisational behaviour in the Weatherhead School of Management, the business school of Case Western Reserve University in Cleveland, Ohio. He received his Ph.D. in social psychology from Harvard in 1967. His research interests are the nature of individual and social change, career development, executive and professional education and experiential learning (adapted from http://www.infed.org/biblio/b-explrn.htm).

Kolb is the author of one of the most important contributions to experiential learning, namely, *Experiential learning: Experience as the source of learning and development* (1984). In 1971 he created the Kolb Learning Style Inventory (LSI) (http://www.learningfromexperience.com/about-us/). In the early 1970s, David Kolb and Roger Fry (both at the Weatherhead School of Management) developed *The Experiential Learning Model* (published in Kolb & Fry, 1975), composed of four elements: concrete experience; reflective observation; abstract conceptualisation; and active experimentation. These four elements form a cycle of learning. Learning can start with any one of the four elements, but typically begins with a concrete experience. The model is strongly related to the earlier work of John Dewey, Jean Piaget, Kurt Lewin and other authors of the Experiential Learning paradigm. The Experiential Learning model was developed originally for designing learning environments in adult education, but is also widely recognised as relevant for higher education. Moreover, Kolb's ideas have influenced corporate training and even kindergarten learning.

Kolb's Experiential Learning Theory

Experiential Learning Theory (ELT) provides a holistic model of the learning process and a multi-linear model of adult development, both of which are consistent with what we know about how people learn, grow and develop (Boyatzis, Kolb, & Mainemelis, 1999, p. 2).

In this theory, experience is the core element in the learning process. The term 'experiential' is used to differentiate ELT both from cognitive learning theories that tend to emphasise cognition over affect, and behavioural learning theories that deny any role for subjective experience in the learning process (ibid.).

As mentioned in *The Kolb Learning Style Inventory – Version 3.1, 2005 Technical Specifications* (Kolb & Kolb, 2005), ELT is based on the work of prominent twentieth-century scholars who gave experience a central role in their theories of human learning and development, notably John Dewey, Kurt Lewin, Jean Piaget, Carl Jung, and Carl Rogers. The theory, described in detail in Kolb (1984), is built on six propositions which these scholars share. The following statement of these propositions is partly literally quoted and partly paraphrased from Kolb and Kolb (2005, p. 194):

1   Learning is best understood as a process, not in terms of the outcomes. To improve learning in higher education, the primary focus should be on engaging students in a process that best enhances their learning, a process that includes feedback on the effectiveness of their learning efforts. As John Dewey said (1916, p. 1): 'education must be conceived as a continuing reconstruction of experience: the process and goal of education are one and the same thing.'

2   All learning is relearning. Learning is best facilitated by a process that draws out the students' beliefs and ideas about a topic, so that they can be examined, tested and integrated with new, more refined ideas.

3   Learning requires the resolution of conflicts between dialectically opposed modes of adaptation to the world. Conflict, differences and disagreement are what drive the learning process. In the process of learning, one is called upon to move back and forth between opposing modes of reflection, action, feeling and thinking.

4   Learning is a holistic process of adaptation to the world. It is not just the result of cognition, but involves the integrated functioning of the total person: thinking, feeling, perceiving and behaving.

5   Learning results from synergetic transactions between the person and the environment. According to Piaget, learning occurs through equilibration of two dialectic processes: assimilating new experiences into existing concepts and accommodating existing concepts to new experience.

6   Learning is the process of creating knowledge. ELT proposes a constructivist theory of learning, whereby social knowledge is created and recreated in the personal knowledge of the learner. This stands in contrast to the 'transmission' model, on which much current educational practice is based, where pre-existing fixed ideas are transmitted to the learner.

The Experiential Learning Model

Experiential Learning Theory defines learning as 'the process whereby knowledge is created through the transformation of experience. Knowledge results from the combination of grasping and transforming experience' (Kolb, 1984, p. 41). The ELT model portrays two dialectically related modes of *grasping* experience – Concrete Experience (CE) and Abstract Conceptualisation (AC) – and two dialectically related modes of *transforming* experience – Reflective Observation (RO) and Active Experimentation (AE) (ibid.). Kolb and Fry (1975) argue that effective learning entails the possession of these four abilities. But few of us can become experts in all four, so we tend to develop a strength in, or orientation towards, one of the poles of each dimension (http://www.infed.org/biblio/b-explrn.htm). According to the four-stage learning cycle depicted in Figure 4.1 (Kolb, 1984), immediate or *concrete experiences* (a person carrying out a particular action and then seeing the effect of the action in *this* situation) are the basis for observations and *reflections* (to understand the effect *in the particular instance*). After deriving *the general principle* behind the effect of the action from which new implications for action can be drawn, these reflections are assimilated and distilled into *abstract concepts*. These implications can be *actively tested* in a range of circumstances and serve as guides in creating new experiences. Two aspects can be seen as especially noteworthy: the use of concrete, *'here-and-now' experience* to test ideas, and the use of *feedback* to change practices and theories (ibid., pp. 21–22).

The ELT model suggests that learning requires abilities that are polar opposites. In each learning situation the learner must choose which set of learning abilities he or she will use. The CE ability refers to learners who grasp experience by perceiving new information through hands-on experience, and thereby relying on senses and feelings. We can call this method sensational. The AC ability involves perceiving, grasping and holding new information through symbolic representation or *abstract conceptualisation*. It is about thinking, analysing or systematically planning, rather than relying on senses and feelings. Similarly, in *transforming* or *processing*

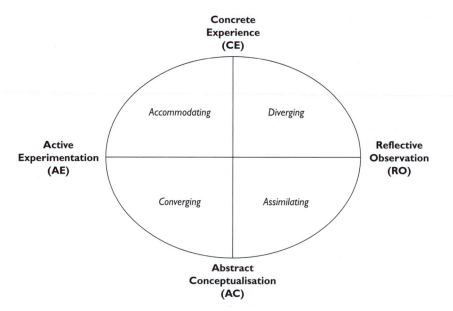

Figure 4.1 The experiential learning cycle and basic learning styles (Kolb, 1984).

experience, some learners choose immediate action (*active experimentation*), others observe people involved in an experience and reflect on what is happening (*reflective observation*) (Boyatzis *et al.*, 1999).

Since we cannot use both modes of grasping and transforming at the same time in a particular situation, we are forced to choose. This is well illustrated in the following example: it is virtually impossible to simultaneously ride your new professional bicycle (Concrete Experience) and analyse the manual about how to use the gears (Abstract Conceptualisation), so we resolve the conflict by choosing. ELT states that learners develop a preferred way of choosing, based on individual genetics, past life experiences and how they perceive the demands of the present environment. They resolve the conflict between concrete and abstract, and between active and reflective in some patterned, characteristic ways. We call these patterned ways '*learning styles*' (ibid.).

While individuals tested on the LSI show many different score patterns, research on the instrument has identified four statistically prevalent learning styles – Diverging, Assimilating, Converging, and Accommodating.[1]

The *Diverging* style's dominant learning abilities are Concrete Experience (CE) and Reflective Observation (RO). Kolb and Kolb (2005, p. 196) define this style as follows: 'People with this learning style learn best by viewing concrete situations from many different angles. It is labelled "Diverging" because this style performs better in situations that call for a generation of ideas, such as "brainstorming" sessions.'

The *Assimilating* style's dominant learning abilities are Abstract Conceptualisation (AC) and Reflective Observation (RO). According to Kolb and Kolb (ibid.): 'People with this learning style are best at understanding a wide range of information and putting it into a concise, logical form. Individuals with an Assimilating style are less focused on people and more interested in ideas and abstract concepts.'

The *Converging* style's dominant learning abilities are Abstract Conceptualisation (AC) and Active Experimentation (AE). Learners with this learning style are good in problem-solving and decision-making by finding practical solutions to questions or problems through the use of ideas and theories: 'Individuals with a Converging learning style prefer to deal with technical tasks and problems rather than with social and interpersonal issues' (ibid.).

The *Accommodating* style's dominant learning abilities are Concrete Experience (CE) and Active Experimentation (AE). The learners characterised by this learning style have the ability to 'learn primarily by "hands-on" experience' (ibid.). In solving problems they rely on their social networks for information rather than on their own technical analysis.

Kolb's LSI has not found widespread popularity, whereas the Experiential Learning paradigm has. One of the problems with the LSI is the assumption of learning *styles*, which implicates a predetermination perspective on the way individuals learn. New perspectives on learning – from Säljö and Entwistle, for example – interpret the patterned way in which individuals learn as *strategies*, rather than inherent styles. People *learn* to learn in a certain way, using different learning strategies and developing their learning strategy according to the context rather than as a result of a personality trait. People take a different approach to how they study depending on the perceived demands of the context where they work and undertake learning activities.

Boud's experiential learning

> Tell me, and I will forget.
> Show me, and I may remember.
> Involve me, and I will understand.
>   (Confucius, 450 BC)

Professor David Boud is a leading educational scientist in the Faculty of Education, University of Technology, Sydney, Australia. His contribution to the current understanding of experience-based learning – experiential learning – and the role of reflection in learning, earned him the reputation of being one of the all-time greats in the field of adult learning. Besides his other specialties – workplace learning, autonomy in learning and problem-based learning – the main focus of this chapter is on his contributions and theories on experience-based learning.

Although Kolb (1984) has recognised 'observations and reflections' as one of the four components in his Experiential Learning model, there is some criticism that he paid insufficient attention to reflection in his broader theory. Boud and Walker (1990), in addressing the question 'What can be done to enhance the possibility of learning occurring in any given situation?', identified reflection as one of the key processes in learning from experience. They further elaborated on the notion that learning can be enhanced by learners employing methods by which they can focus attention on events and extract meaning from their experiences through a variety of reflective activities.

Some of the key findings in this regard were documented by Boud, Keogh and Walker (1985a). The focus of that work was on reflection following experience, rather than reflection during experience. They further proposed a model for reflection and offered various strategies for reflecting on experience. The key elements of this model were 'return to experience', 'attending to feelings' and 're-evaluation of the experience', each of which was elaborated on in some detail.

> *Returning to experience* is simply the recollection of the salient events, the replaying of the initial experience in the mind of the learner or the recounting to others of the features of the experience.
>
>   (Ibid., p. 27, emphasis added)

> *Attending to (or connecting with) feelings* consists of the utilisation of positive feelings, involving focusing on positive feelings about learning and the experience which is subject to reflection, and removing obstructing feelings, which may involve expressing one's feelings when recounting an event to

others by, for example, laughing during the telling of an embarrassing incident or by some other form of catharsis.

(Ibid., p. 33, emphasis added)

Evaluating experience involves re-examining in the light of the learner's intent, associating new knowledge into the learner's conceptual framework and also involves a rehearsal in which the new learning is applied mentally to test its authenticity and the planning of subsequent activity in which this learning is applied in one's life.

(Ibid., p. 30, emphasis added)

Addressing these issues further, Boud and Walker (1990) focused their attention on how to learn through experiences, how learners can influence the experience and consequently their own learning and how others might facilitate such learning from experience. Restricting their concern to (a) deliberate learning, i.e., the learner has an intention to learn from experience (Dewey, 1916; Tough, 1979), and (b) meaningful learning, i.e., learning is intended to be applied meaningfully by the learner (cf. Usher's (1985) thematised approach), some authors sketched a practical framework, for use by learners and those who facilitate learning, which focuses on key elements of the process of learning from experience. They also showed that a greater awareness of what is happening in, and a more deliberate interaction with, the learning milieu will provide greater opportunities for a more fruitful learning experience. There is no necessary correspondence between awareness of these interactions and learning. Nevertheless, one would expect that such awareness can help equip learners with a framework that can help them begin to appreciate the complex dynamics of the situations with which they are confronted. Awareness is definitely necessary, but it is not enough; raising awareness enhances learning opportunities.

Boud and Walker (1990) considered experience as an interaction between a learner and a social, psychological and material environment or milieu. There is potential for learning in every situation and it is up to the learner to realise this potential. It is the learner's interaction with the learning milieu that creates the particular learning experience. While facilitators and others can help create the milieu, it is the learner who creates the experience. It can be helpful to distinguish between the *event* and the *experience*. The event is the whole situation as observed by someone detached from it, whereas the experience is the situation as it is known and lived by the learner. Reflection on experience, understood in this way, will focus on understanding the learner and the learning environment or milieu, and on the interaction that takes place between the two.

In summary, the work of Boud and Walker (ibid.) on reflection, as shown in Figure 4.2, is as follows. Reflection is grounded in the learner's *personal foundation of experience*, that is, those experiences that have shaped the person and have helped create the person he or she is now, and their *intent* that gives a particular focus to their learning in any particular context. Learning occurs through the interaction

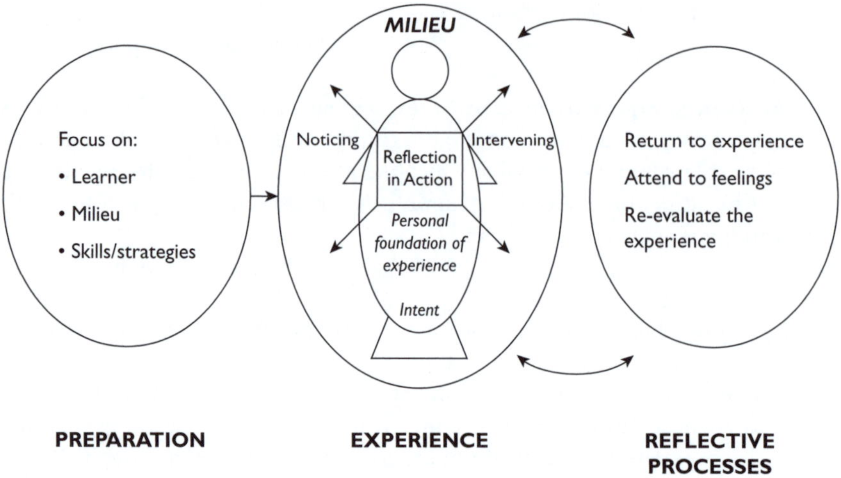

Figure 4.2 Reflection: the personal foundation of experience (from Boud & Walker, 1990).

of the person with his or her material and the human environment (*the learning milieu*); it is assisted through the learners giving attention to (*noticing*) what is happening within themselves and in their external environment; *intervening* in various ways to influence themselves and the milieu in which they are operating; and reflecting-in-action to continually modify their noticing and interventions. The model suggests that there are an endless number of reflective strategies that might be adopted, but those that are chosen must be related to the needs and intent of the learners and the nature of the milieu.

First we will describe the main ideas as described by Boud and Walker (1990): the learner, intent, the learning milieu and the learning experience.

The learner

When the learner enters a new experience, he brings with him the presuppositions and assumptions developed in the past which are, as Usher (1989, p. 32) argues, 'situated within the social world of discursive contexts.'

The accumulation of these prior experiences predisposes the learner toward any future experience. In this respect, Boud and Walker (1990) refer to the personal foundation of experience:

'The learner possesses a personal foundation of experience, a way of being present in the world, which profoundly influences the way it is experienced and which will particularly influence the intellectual and emotional content of the experience and the meanings that are attributed to it . . . (the personal foundation of experience)' is partly acquired from the social and cultural environment, and partly forged by the learner's own awareness and effort.

(p. 62)

However, as Boud and Walker (1990) argue, during the event itself, learners are not always aware of the personal foundation of their experience. Reflections on it may elicit the origin of their thoughts, feelings and actions.

Intent

Boud and Walker (1990, p. 63) define intent 'as a personal determination that provides a particular orientation within a given situation, a rationale for why the learner comes to the particular learning event. Intent is the foundation for self-directed learning; it prompts learners to take steps to achieve their goals.'

Learning intent influences the way learners experience events. It is the intent that acts as magnifier or a filter: it focuses and intensifies the perception of the learner in relation to certain parts of an experience, or (sometimes at the same time) plays down or eliminates others.

The intent of the learner can be influenced by his core values and ideals, especially when entering an experience that appeals to general life intents 'such as the desire for success and recognition, or personal, religious or political commitments' (Boud and Walker, 1990, p. 63). However, in other situations, the intent of the learner is a pragmatic response to a situation.

Boud and Walker (1990) argue that the learner is not always aware of a particular intent. In those situations, the learner's intent can be observed from the actions, thoughts or feelings that result from it. Here again, reflection after the event is a valuable tool to make the learner aware of his intent.

However, Boud and Walker (1990, pp. 63–64) argue that 'the nature of learning from experience is such that intent never acts as the sole arbiter of outcomes: the learner has but partial control over events and, while he or she may become more adept in dealing with them, the world provides its own challenges to continually provoke and stimulate the learner.'

The learning milieu

Every situation the learner enters can be a learning milieu. Boud and Walker (1990, p. 64) define the learning milieu in the formal educational setting as 'the socio-psychological and material environment in which students and teachers work together . . . [it] represents a network or nexus of cultural, social, institutional and psychological variables. These interact in complicated ways to produce, in each class or course, a unique pattern of circumstances, pressures, customs, opinions and work styles, which suffuse the teaching and learning that occur there.' In this environment, student and teachers are learners and facilitators; the classes and programs or courses offer opportunities for the learner to learn.

The notion of milieu is not only limited to formal learning situations but also applies to informal learning situations. This aforementioned definition of Boud and Walker (1990) captures the complexity of the learning milieu. It indicates that the milieu is not only the physical environment where learning takes place. 'It embraces the formal requirements, the culture, procedures, practices and standards of certain institutions and societies, the immediate goals and expectations of any facilitator, as well as the personal characteristics of individuals who are part of it' (Boud and Walker, 1990, p. 64). Moreover, it includes all human and material entities that provide the context and events within which the learner operates: 'the immediate players who happen to be present. They include the history, values and ideologies of the culture, as well as the manifestations of these in particular events. Issues such as gender, race and class are all potentially significant elements of the milieu.' (p. 66) Boud and Walker specifically focus on the interaction between the learner and the milieu. Learning is a function of the relationship between the learner and the milieu and is never something determined by one of those elements alone (Entwistle, Hounsell, & Marton, 1984).

The learning experience

It is the aforementioned interaction between learner and milieu and more precisely the learner's engagement with the milieu that constitutes the particular learning experience. As Boud and Walker explain (1990, p. 65): 'The milieu becomes the context of learning by virtue of the learner's entry into it. Each learner forms part of the milieu, enriching it with his or her personal contribution and creating an interaction that is the learning experience for him or herself and for others.'

Both authors stress that the learner is part of the milieu as a reflective person, 'being able to stand back or withdraw from the immediate interaction to become aware of what is taking place, and to dialogue with it . . . The learners' construction of what is taking place within themselves and within the milieu is a necessary and crucial part of the ongoing experience and the learning that flows from it. It is this interaction that lies at the heart of the ongoing experience.' (p. 65)

In sum, the experience is defined by Boud and Walker (1990) as 'a continuing, complex series of interactions between the learner and the learning milieu, unified by reflective processes that assimilate and work with the learning potential of the environment, and can move the learner to take appropriate action within the experience' (p. 65) (see Figure 4.2).

Boud and Walker stress that reflective processes can take place during, as well as after, the experience. Reflection includes that the learner returns to the experience handles the feelings that arise and re-evaluates the experience, 'which involves the association of new data with previous learning, the processing and integrating of these associations and the testing of what is learned' (Boud and Walker, 1990, p. 65).

Reflective processes only can work when two conditions are met. First, the person has to become aware of the milieu, or particular things within it, using this for the focus of reflection. Boud and Walker (1990) refer to this condition as 'noticing'. 'Noticing is essential to the initiation of the reflective process and can provide further evidence on which to reflect' (p. 65).

Second, the person has to take an initiative in the event, called '*intervening*'. Intervening may imply an attempt to change the event, in a major or minor way, or to check if he understands what is happening. When the learner intervenes in an event, this may lead to a change of the event so that the learner needs to look at it again.

Boud and Walker (1990) argue that there can be a continuing cycle of noticing, reflecting, intervening, noticing, reflecting; however, there can also be many combinations of these activities interspersed with each other, which may appear to have no link with the learning task.

However, noticing, intervening as well as reflection are crucial to learning.

Applications in the workplace

David Kolb's theory is widely applied in many fields from education to business. It has gained popularity because of its practical good results in various structures. The findings on ELT indicate that it has helped students to become self-aware (see, e.g., Bradbeer, 1999), has assisted staff in becoming reflective teachers (see, e.g., Burkill, Corey, & Healey, 2000), has identified students' learning styles to facilitate the selection of mixed groups (see, e.g., Hertzog & Lieble, 1996), has helped to develop and teach key skills (see, e.g., Chalkley & Harwood, 1998; Haigh & Kilmartin, 1999) and helped to design group project work (see, e.g., Brown, 1999; Mellor, 1991). In view of the research into learning from experience, the number of its advocates is constantly increasing.

The theory has found widespread application in many fields and is used for teams as well as for individuals. Tools such as fieldwork, laboratory sessions, role-plays, case studies, journals and problem-solving exercises are used to help learners critically reflect on what is being learned. What is important is to *systematically take the learner around each stage of the cycle*, ensuring that effective links are made between each stage.

Back to the case study

Analysing the virtual simulation exercise of the Emergency Management Team from Kolb's Experiential Learning Cycle, indicates that the following steps are taken:

1   *Concrete experience*: the exercise starts with scenario 1 and the Commanders do their job: they explore the scene, develop an image of the situation and initialise and conduct a multidisciplinary meeting.

2   *Reflective observation*: after the first meeting the trainer takes a time-out and evaluates the first meeting with the Commanders. Together they reflect on what happened, what went well and what can be done better next time.

3   *Abstract conceptualisation*: together the Commanders define what worked and what did not in terms of procedures and actions, and make a plan for what to do next time.

4   *Active experimentation*: the new or adapted procedures and actions are *actively tested* in new scenarios and serve as guides in creating new experiences.

Based on the active experimentation in new scenarios, the Commanders on Scene gain new experiences, on which they reflect again. Here the learning cycle starts again.

In this case, there is not only reflection after playing the scenario, but the trainer can decide to stop the simulation at any time that he decides reflection is needed. This implies reflection during and after the experience (Boud, 1988).

As part of the reflection, trainers encourage the trainees to return to the experience, by asking them what has happened and with what consequences? This refers to the issue of noticing, as Boud argued for. Attention is paid to the Commanders' personal foundation of experience and their intent in terms of values and norms (different values and norms can lead to a difference in decisions taken in the emergency case).

Note

1   The enumeration of the different learning styles has been taken from *The Kolb Learning Style Inventory – Version 3.1, 2005 Technical Specifications* (Kolb & Kolb, 2005), with some minor adaptations.

References

Boud, D. (ed.) (1988). *Developing student autonomy in learning* (2nd edn). London: Kogan Page.

Boud, D., & Walker, D. (1990). 'Making the most of experience', *Studies in Continuing Education*, 12(2), 61–80.

Boud, D., Keogh, R., & Walker, D. (eds) (1985a). *Reflection: Turning experience into learning*. London: Kogan Page.

Boud, D., Keogh, R., & Walker, D. (1985b). 'Promoting reflection in learning: a model', in D. Boud, R. Keogh, & D. Walker (eds), *Reflection: Turning experience into learning* (pp. 18–40). London: Kogan Page.

Boyatzis, R. E., Kolb, D. A., & Mainemelis, C. (1999). 'Experiential learning theory: Previous research and new directions', in R. J. Sternberg, & L. F. Zhang (eds), *Perspectives on cognitive learning and thinking styles*. Mahwah, NJ: Lawrence Erlbaum.

Bradbeer, J. (1999). 'Barriers to interdisciplinarity: Disciplinary discourses and student learning', *Journal of Geography in Higher Education*, 23(3), 381–396.

Brown, G. H. (1999). 'A group-learning approach to academic and transferable skills through an exercise in the global positioning system', *Journal of Geography in Higher Education*, 23(3), 291–301.

Burkill, S., Corey, D., & Healey, M. (2000). *Improving students' communication skills in geography.* Cheltenham: Geography Discipline Network, Cheltenham and Gloucester College of Higher Education.

Chalkley, B., & Harwood, J. (1998). *Transferable skills and work-based learning in geography.* Cheltenham: Geography Discipline Network, Cheltenham and Gloucester College of Higher Education.

Dewey, J. (1916). *Democracy and education.* New York: Macmillan.

Entwistle, N., Hounsell, D., & Marton, F. (1984). *The experience of learning.* Edinburgh: Scottish Academic Press.

Haigh, M., & Kilmartin, M. P. (1999). 'Student perceptions of the development of personal transferable skills', *Journal of Geography in Higher Education*, 23(2), 195–206.

Hertzog, C. J., & Lieble, C. (1996). 'A study of two techniques for teaching introductory geography: Traditional approach versus cooperative learning in the university classroom', *Journal of Geography*, 95(6), 274–280.

Knowles, M. S. (1975). *Self-directed learning: A guide for learners and teachers.* New York: Association Press.

Kolb, D. A. (1984). *Experiential learning: Experience as the source of learning and development.* Englewood Cliffs, NJ: Prentice-Hall.

Kolb. D. A., & Fry, R. (1975) 'Toward an applied theory of experiential learning', in C. Cooper (ed.), *Theories of Group Process.* London: John Wiley.

Kolb, D. A., & Kolb A. (2005). *The Kolb Learning Style Inventory – Version 3.1, 2005 Technical Specifications.* Retrieved 10 April 2008 from http://www.learningfrom experience.com/images/uploads/Tech_spec_LSI.pdf.

Mellor, A. (1991). 'Experiential learning through integrated project work: An example from soil science', *Journal of Geography in Higher Education*, 15(2), 135–149.

Rogers, C. R. (1983). *Freedom to learn in the 80's.* Columbus, OH: Charles E. Merrill.

Tough, A. (1979). *The adult's learning projects* (2nd edn). Toronto: Ontario Institute for Studies in Education.

Usher, R. S. (1985). 'Beyond the anecdotal: Adult learning and the use of experience', *Studies in the Education of Adults*, 17(1), 59–74.

Usher, R. S. (1989). 'Locating experience in language: Towards a poststructuralist theory of experience', *Adult Education Quarterly*, 40(1), 23–32.

Wikipedia, the Free Encyclopaedia (2008). *David A. Kolb.* Retrieved 9 April 2008 from http://en.wikipedia.org/wiki/David_A._Kolb.

Chapter 5

From the theory of situated cognition to communities of practice: J. Lave and E. Wenger

Stephen Hargreaves and David Gijbels

Case study: the Virtual English Teaching Community

Four years ago a virtual team to support English language trainers in their ICT and communication skills was created: the Virtual English Teaching Community (VET). A group of highly ICT-oriented secondary and higher education teachers that met virtually were also physically brought together and driven to share their expertise relating to teaching English supported by ICT. Introducing a 'community of practice' based on the Wikipedia model is what this team is modestly aiming at. Current standings, however, indicate a low achievement status by its members and although an enormous amount of communicative and multimedia oriented exercises have been put online, mostly by the four administrators, its 400+ registered users show a high free-riding mentality, i.e., picking up materials without sharing their own. It seems that only a small proportion of these teams reach a satisfactory level of performance (Kimble, Li, & Barlow, 2000). The VET community is a share-point for all members of an Antwerp school community. Its aim is to develop a useful database including, for example, lesson materials, ideas, proposals, documents, projects, school trip reports, all of which have been put together by (all) English teachers. The real quality of such a project equals the productivity of the broad layer, i.e., the participating teachers. The structure includes the foundation, i.e., the teachers who are scattered all over the Antwerp school community, locally organised in school-oriented communities of practice (CoP). Every local CoP has an anchor teacher who heads the local community and is responsible for material upload. The coordinator heads all anchor teachers and cares for the maintenance and upload of the VET CoP. Three times per school year the coordinator organises a school surpassing community meeting with all anchor teachers. This cycle includes the following actions:

1   September: meeting fellow colleagues, planning of the actions and aims, brainstorming . . .
2   January: evaluation of the first semester, new ideas for coming semester, evaluation of the CoP, ad hoc actions . . .
3   May/June: review past school year, forecast new year, evaluation, suggest new ideas for further action and growth.

Mechanisms

The CoP has a bipolar approach. The first part has to do with sharing materials. All supersonic lesson materials produced by every individual teacher must not stay on individual islands. Take into account the following statements: colleague W is a master in making complicated grammar look and feel digestible; colleague X is extremely creative when dealing with vocabulary; colleague Y builds cleverly designed reading and listening exercises; colleague Z has just finished the London project.

Putting all these W, X, Y and Z colleagues together creates the 'perfect' English teacher if they are willing to *share* all their knowledge, skills and attitudes (KSAs). Weak spot in your KSAs? Lack of time? Other priorities? All the aforementioned issues may block your aspirations of creating something with, for example, ICT. The CoP could be your helpline. Budding teachers, new teachers, just remember how difficult our own professional career was. Curricula, school plans, lesson plans, exercise books, reference books all have a link with the CoP. Learning how to share is something a child doesn't do spontaneously. It has to be taught step by step. A child knows very quickly what is *his*, but it is a lot more complicated to grasp that other children can *have* too. This doesn't mean that your child is selfish. Someone who works alone adds knowledge, someone who shares and works together multiplies it. This clearly indicates the difference between the addition approach and the multiplication model.

The second foundation of the CoP is centralisation of content. All important documents and information are only three clicks away. It has an agenda where all activities are posted in a user-friendly way; links to a lot of interesting URLs; administration of curricula, proceedings, minutes, meetings; announcements to communicate precious ideas; reactions to support all contributors and give positive and honest feedback.

All activities were started up little by little; all CoP members are part of the school community. Physical and virtual feedback moments are organised on a frequent basis and as every school has an anchor teacher the CoP itself is very approachable. The CoPs comprise part of an official plan of action devised by all board members of the school community. The sharing of content has been integrated in the official VLE, used by all schools in the community.

How does it work?

Once you have logged in to the platform what you see as a member of the community is displayed in Figure 5.1. The document folder (Figure 5.2) holds all the lesson plans and is organised around split-class teaching. It contains multimedia enhanced lessons with focus on form (FonF), communicative teaching and self-sustained learning activities such as WebQuests. Teachers are free to use all of the materials and evaluate them (feedback). All exercises are organised first according to the four skills (reading, writing, listening and speaking), second according to the Flemish 3X2 system (three grades, each grade two school years) with an advanced, intermediate and beginners tag.

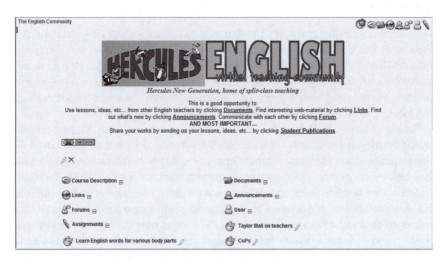

Figure 5.1 ELOvanA platform 1 (from www.ELOvanA.be).

The English Community > Documents > Home

Type	Name	Size ↓	Date
📄	How to register at the VET community	💾 538k	2 years, 4 months 2008-01-07 16:11:20
📄	affiche ELOvanA-dag	💾 116.63k	1 year, 7 months 2008-09-17 20:39:01
📁	Multimedia projects enhancing split-class teaching ACE, Anglia, CD Rom material, WebQuest-workshops	💾 12.67M	2 years, 4 months 2008-01-10 13:59:16
📁	VET Community - practice, lessons, ... Virtual English Teaching Community - class material	💾 25.77M	1 year, 8 months 2008-08-26 20:18:35
📁	VET Community - documentation Virtual English Teaching Community - methodology	💾 31.03M	1 year, 8 months 2008-09-03 09:09:55

Figure 5.2 ELOvanA platform 2 (from www.ELOvanA.be).

Introduction

Fundamental changes have taken place in the education environment which force teachers and organisations to utilise new technology, generally under the ICT umbrella. It goes without saying that implementing ICT in secondary schools is a slow and frustrating process. Many problems stem from a lack of understanding of ICT and a quasi non-existent pedagogical framework resulting in a slow and mostly technology-driven approach in schools. A crucial element in positive ICT implementation seems to be the professionalism of teachers. The relationship between ICT benefits and the degree of the teachers' ICT integration during teaching has been clearly indicated in review studies (Becta, 2006; Cox, 2004; Drent, 2005). The teacher has a crucial part in the ICT output. The introduction of ICT in learning in general seems to be missing a backbone which should be offered by education oriented organisations. Teachers are mostly left on their own when it comes to looking for and implementing good practices in their micro environment, i.e., their classrooms.

In Flanders and The Netherlands there are excellent initiatives, for example, Kennisnet, Klascement, Anywize, Pienternet, ELOvanA (all sponsored by Flemish federal or local subsidies). The problem, however, is their general approach of only trying to reach a broad group of teachers without focusing on mutual community networking. Lesson editing, transfer of materials, meta-tagging, sharing knowledge, exchanging interesting lesson plans, these activities are not effective without CoP. Most initiatives seem to lack the boost of sharing materials mutually. It is presented as a return ticket system, but nevertheless one stands with a single ticket. Everybody is keen to collect useful materials; sharing and improving them is something quite different. Groups that are formed to share what they know and to learn from one another regarding some aspects of their work are labelled as CoPs. Such groups have been around ever since people in organisations realised they could benefit from sharing their knowledge, insights and experiences with others who have similar interests or goals. Through networking and sharing experiences, particularly the problems teachers encounter and the solutions they devise, a core group of these teachers proved extremely effective in improving their lessons' efficiency and effectiveness using ICT materials. The impact on students' awareness, communication, social skills, motivation and competencies in general planted the seeds of the anytime-anywhere learning model and lifelong learning.

In education and elsewhere, people create and apply knowledge. In education, where KSAs of learning should be in peak condition, we have the feeling that knowledge is formed like an addition and not as a multiplication. Teachers do not always have the inclination to learn from one another, let alone learn from students or learners. Multiplication of knowledge is possible where mechanisms like CoPs have been introduced in the school system or school community, picking up learners with common interests, such as how to more effectively use ICT. In order to work effectively in 'digital education' school communities are looking for supportive tools. CoPs are seen as flexible and effective means of bringing both teachers' skills and expertise to bear on specific problems. Since teachers are spread all over the country, working in a 'distributed environment', the danger is that teams will lose many of the opportunities for informal collaboration and knowledge sharing (Kimble *et al.*, 2000). Networking seems to be a complicated business in a scattered Flemish education system (catholic schools, state schools and a miscellaneous group of smaller school organisers).

The theory: from situated cognition to Communities of Practice

Lave and Wenger first introduced the concept of a CoP in 1991 in their book, *Situated cognition: Legitimate peripheral participation*. The theory of 'situated cognition' emerged as a result of dissatisfaction with the asocial character of conventional learning theory and its inability to account for how people learn new activities and acquire knowledge and skills without engagement in formal educational or training processes (Fuller, Hodkinson, Hodkinson, & Unwin, 2005, p. 50). Central in their theory is the idea that learning is an integral and inseparable aspect of social practice (Lave & Wenger, 1991, p. 31). It means that all learning processes are embedded in social interactions among people and in the context where socialising occurs. Moreover, according to Lave and Wenger learning is not only situated in practice but is a part of it in the real world. In addition, learning involves the whole person and construction of identities (ibid., p. 53), which means that, during the learning process, personality is under constant change.

In other words, Lave and Wenger see the acquisition of knowledge as a social process where people can participate in communal learning at different levels depending on their level of authority or seniority in the group, i.e., whether they are a newcomer or have been a member for a long time. In this context, the notion of 'legitimate peripheral participation' is used to capture the insight that learners inevitably participate in communities of practitioners and that the mastery of knowledge and skill requires newcomers to move toward full participation in the sociocultural practices of the community (ibid.). Legitimate peripheral participation (LPP) means in other words that learning is seen as a situated activity in social practice (ibid.). LPP is not in itself an educational form, much less a pedagogical strategy or a teaching technique. It is an analytical viewpoint on learning, a way of understanding learning (ibid., p. 40). LPP happens in a community where knowledge is not decontextualised like in schools. LPP means that when an apprentice starts his learning as a newcomer, he observes and works together with an old-timer (experienced worker or master) and gradually, as his participation increases, he becomes an old-timer himself (ibid.). It means that old-timers accept the presence of newcomers (legitimacy) and their participation is peripheral while they learn the skills necessary to become full members of the community of practice. Lave and Wenger (ibid., p. 53) go on to say that LPP means that learning is not merely a condition for membership, but is itself an evolving form of membership. In addition, they (ibid., p. 55) see LPP as a bridge between changing persons and changing communities of practice. The key to LPP is newcomers' access to the community of practice being the same as the old-timers (ibid.). Nevertheless, newcomers have fewer demands on time, effort and responsibility (ibid.). The authors also mention that social interaction between newcomers and old-timers involves relations of power.

Lave and Wenger have developed the concept of 'community of practice' to convey how people learn through mutual engagement in an activity which is defined by the negotiation of meanings both inside and outside the community. They argue that: 'A community of practice is a set of relations among persons, activity, and world, over time and in relation to other tangential and overlapping communities of practice' (ibid., p. 40). CoPs share and form knowledge on the basis of pull by individual members, not on the basis of a centralised push of information. Knowledge-based strategies need to create a mechanism for practitioners to reach out to other practitioners rather than to focus on gathering and distributing information. Teacher trainers and teachers should set high performance aspirations and then create tools, systems and incentives together with school managers so that the exchange of ideas and solutions is facilitated and practitioners can solve problems together (Manville & Foote, 1996). Learning about practice doesn't make you become a better practitioner. Becoming a better practitioner, not learning about practice is the central issue in learning. This approach draws attention away from abstract and theoretical knowledge and detailed processes and situates it in the communities and practices in which knowledge takes on significance (Seely Brown & Duguid, 1996). Teachers could be more motivated to apply ICT as a result because tasks and exercises could be developed in a collaborative way, i.e., together, and tested and classified as cut-and-dried, ready-to-use materials.

CoPs are an integral and seemingly trivial part of our daily lives. They are so familiar and informal to us that they rarely come into explicit focus. While the experience is not new, the label 'communities of practice' has been used only recently. Most CoPs do not have a specific name or membership cards. Nevertheless, it would not be difficult for us to construct a relatively good picture of the CoPs we have belonged to in the past, we belong to at present and those we would like to belong to in the future if we consider our own life from that perspective for a moment. Even more, although membership is rarely made explicit on a list and no check-list for qualifying criteria exists, we also have a pretty good idea of who belongs to our CoPs and why. And even further, it would not be difficult for us to distinguish between a few CoPs of which we have a peripheral kind of membership and a number of others in which we belong to the core members (Wenger, 1998). To illustrate, Manville and Foote (1996, p. 10) offer the following definition of a CoP: '. . . a group of professionals informally bound to one another through exposure to a common class of problems [and] common pursuit of solutions and thereby themselves embodying a store of knowledge'. Seely Brown and Solomon Gray (1995, p. 3) suggest:

> At the simplest level, they are a small group of people who have worked together over a period of time. Not a team, not a task force, not necessarily an authorised or identified group – They are peers in the execution of 'real work'. What holds them together is a common sense of purposes and a real need to know what the others know.

Reflections on the theory based on the Virtual English Teaching Community experience

Virtual and physical CoPs, trust and identity

CoPs provide mechanisms for overcoming some of the technological, organisational and cultural barriers. Key aspects of successful CoPs are trust and identity. The creation of new electronic environments that coexist with the physical environment in which practitioners, often in teams, operate, also creates new barriers to the effective functioning of virtual teams. To understand the barriers to virtual teams it is necessary to examine the main features of the new virtual environment and its relationship to the physical environment. An essential element in which virtual teams differ from others is that they operate in and make use of an electronic space. The emergence of the electronic space however does not decrease the significance of the physical space as many characteristics of the physical space will continue to affect the development and operation of organisations (Kimble *et al.*, 2000). In a changing and less stable organisation the issues of trust and identity are as crucial for the effective formation and functioning of virtual teams as they are for non virtual teams. The importance of trust in the success of teams is highlighted by many others (e.g., Van den Bossche, 2006). Without trust the management of a virtual organisation cannot be conceived:

> Trust is the heart of the matter. That seems obvious and trite yet most of our organisations tend to be arranged on the assumption that people cannot be trusted or relied on even in tiny matters. If we are to enjoy the efficiencies and other benefits of the virtual organisation we will have to rediscover how to run organisations based more on trust than on control. Virtuality requires trust to make it work: technology on its own is not enough.
>
> (Handy, 1995, in Kimble *et al.*, 2000, p. 5)

A shared commitment still requires personal contact to make it real.

The virtual paradox

The more virtual an organisation becomes, the more its people need to meet in person. The 'real life' meetings however are different in nature and are less about tasks and more about the process and about to get to know each other. More than the virtual level, the physical one seems to be important to achieve trust. Jarvenpaa and Leidner (1998) conducted an interesting study about the creation and maintenance of trust in global virtual teams whose members transcend time, space and culture. Jarvenpaa and Leidner noted that those teams that were not focused on a task reported low levels of trust. At the early stages of the virtual teams, greater trust was developed through a balanced mix of task communication and social talk. In the longer term, teams that developed set patterns of communication and responded promptly to other team members generated greater trust. They concluded that the communication that 'rallies around the project or task' appears to be necessary to maintain trust. Informal contact between colleagues, the sharing of projects, solving problems together, the informal swapping of experiences and learning from discussions are examples of typical behaviour to maintain trust.

Members in a virtual CoP can meet on a regular basis (e.g. monthly). In between these meetings they maintain communication via e-mail, telephone, VLE (Virtual Learning Environment) forums and so on. During the periods of electronic communication it is felt that the momentum of the group gradually slows, until a physical meeting revives it. Meetings in the 'real world' allow members to get to know each other far better than in electronic meetings. It is regarded as essential to have a good personal relationship with the other members, as this carries the community through the periods of electronic communication. The personal relationships are needed if members are to go the extra half mile for someone. The above indicates clearly the continued importance of the physical space as it can sustain relationships through subsequent electronic communication (Kimble *et al.*, 2000).

CoP barriers

With the rapid development and implementation of ICT, and the firm establishment of the knowledge-based economy, organisations increasingly have to operate simultaneously in the physical space and in the electronic space:

> At one extreme virtual place in the electronic space is being created enabling people physically located in different places to meet electronically. . . . In essence, space and place have converged into one. . . . Local characteristics will continue to affect the effectiveness of communications between people from different places, even in the 'virtual place'.
>
> (Ibid., p. 5)

The most prevalent technological barriers include the underdevelopment of a telecommunications infrastructure; the demands on expert time in upgrading the systems and for other services and the increasingly growing expectations of users. Working in virtual teams raises problems that are unusual when groups of people work in the physical place. Examples are a lack of nonverbal communication cues, cultural differences between team members and (see also above) problems of trust and identity. The development of a team culture and common communication procedures is essential for a growing trust among team members in a virtual environment (ibid.).

Social and personal implications of CoPs

Hodkinson and Hodkinson (2003) emphasise the social and communal dimensions of learning in education, devoting particular attention to the inter-relationships between the individual workers' dispositions to learning. Two rival metaphors of learning crop up: acquisition versus participation. Lave and Wenger (1991) see learning as a part of the process of becoming a full member. So, learning as participation prioritises the social dimensions of learning. Sometimes learning happens subconsciously, for example, through normal working practices. The separation between the person learning and the context in which they learn can be seen as artificial (Brown, Collins, & Duguid, 1989). In this view, each person is a reciprocal part of the context and learns as such. It is the whole person that interrelates with the social world, and not only the mind. Thinking and learning are embodied (Beckett & Hager, 2002). The embodied person can be seen as constructed through the positioned social life that a person (body and mind) leads, which includes his professional and personal life (Bourdieu, 1984; Bloomer & Hodkinson, 2000). As Hodkinson, Sparkes and Hodkinson (1996) argue, people act or learn within 'horizons for action' and those horizons are simultaneously objective and subjective, depending partly upon the learner's perceptions of the context (e.g., the workplace conditions), as well as the conditions of the context themselves.

Much workplace learning literature focuses primarily upon the workplace itself. Most writers acknowledge the significance of locating individuals within activity systems and/or CoPs.

In an era of accountability and outcome measurement, teachers and school managers are reluctant to leave their classes for their own learning. Therefore, most planned teacher learning activity is located on those days in the year when teachers are in school but pupils are not. Wenger (1998) identifies CoPs as having three dimensions: mutual engagement; joint enterprise; and a shared repertoire of actions, discourses, tools, etc. The community members work closely together. There is a dominant emphasis on the movement from newcomer to old-timer. They share their competence with new generations through a version of the same process by which they develop.

A key characteristic of this community is its continual striving for new and better ways to work. This anticipatory learning (Beckett & Hager, 2002) is the very nature of the practice that determines full membership of this particular community. It is deliberate and incidental, opportunistic and planned, and involves both trial and error judgements. Schools which offer an expansive approach to apprenticeship are more likely to create learning opportunities which foster 'deep learning' (Marton, Hounsell, & Entwistle, 1984), 'investigative deep-level learning' (Engeström, 1994) and 'the work of the imagination' (Wenger, 1998) than they would under a more restrictive approach. We speak of expansive learning, or third-order learning, when a CoP begins to analyse and transform itself. Such expansive learning is not limited to pre-defined contents and tasks anymore. Rather it is a long-term process of redefining the objects, tools and social structures of the workplace (Engeström, 1994). Expansive possibilities for personal development can be enhanced by breaks in routine (Wenger, 1998).

Focus on personal development

The personal development aspect of the CoP is an essential element. This can be fostered through the provision of opportunities to reflect on practice and of opportunities to develop new identities through belonging to a variety of different CoPs. Hodkinson and Hodkinson (2002) argue in their work on the intersection of biography, context and workplace learning, that people's backgrounds and outside interests are highly relevant to their attitudes to learning. This is a reminder that, although important, apprenticeship and work are not the only sources of these young people's attitudes, aspirations and identities. An expansive approach, personal development and identity formation can be seen to include: planned time off the job for reflection and exploration; post-apprenticeship progression – envisioning trajectories, availability of role models; and opportunities for personal development by extending identity through boundary crossing.

Garrick (1998) and Boud (1999) suggest that informal interactions with peers are predominant ways of learning and that the impact of formal training on practice can be quite marginal.

CoP ingredients for success

Issues leading to success in a CoP can be divided into a digital level and a physical level (Hezemans & Ritzen, 2004). Beijering (2002) suggests that the basic functions related to the digital level are: an agenda; folders area; document upload; forum; feedback at document level; full-screen print function; e-mail notification; metadata (tag and search); search engine; planner; invisible/visible key; version administrator; access/authorisation of participants. Basic functions at the physical level (Wenger, McDermott, & Snyder, 2002) include: classifying important issues in the field, organising and preparing CoP meetings, linking CoP members and crossing boundaries between organisation units; observing the evolution of CoP members; observing boundaries between the community and the formal organisation; building up the practice and knowledge basis; assessing the healthiness of the CoP; and assessing the CoP's gain for the members and organisation. People need to share the same problem and solve it together and there is a necessity to do so, driven by intrinsic motivation. Recognising mutual problems helps feed the lively character of a CoP (Hezemans & Ritzen, 2004).

Evaluating is also an important part in the CoP's life cycle. McDermott (2001) outlines the following four steps: of quintessential importance is that management communicates the idea that sharing knowledge is crucial for the organisation

(1); this shared know-how is categorised as 'sharing cutting-edge thinking' (2); the CoP coordinator creates systems to sustain members in their thinking (3); and the personal challenge for members is to be open to other members' new ideas and to further develop community ideas (4).

As mentioned earlier, effects of learning with ICT and in virtual CoPs vary widely. ICT in and of itself cannot transform education. Virtual tools can only provide the information, support certain activities and set the stage for the design of so-called novel learning environments. There is obviously nothing omnipotent about the role of ICT and no real change in and of education (or any other workplace) can take place all on its own (Salomon & Ben-Zvi, 2006). Teachers working together in CoPs are a key element. By focusing on the social dimension and personal growth, combined with a 'common sense of purpose' and the real urge to know what peers know, a CoP is a supernova of intertwining KSAs with class practice in a simultaneous, synchronous and asynchronous physical and virtual setting, topped with trust and identity. Cutting-edge thinking and sharing knowledge are the driving forces behind the CoP principles. Technology on its own is *not* enough. People are the school.

References

Beckett, D., & Hager, P. (2002). *Life, work and learning: Practice in postmodernity.* London: Routledge.

Becta ICT Research (2006). *The Becta review 2006: Evidence on the progress of ICT in education.* Retrieved 25 May 2007 from www.becta.org.uk.

Beijering, J. (2002). *Eindrapport Virtueel Kenniscentrum en expertisenetwerken: Opbouw en verspreiding van expertise* [*Final report on the Virtual Knowledge Centre and expertise networks: accumulation and dissemination of expertise*]. Digitale Universiteit. Retrieved 25 May 2007 from http://www.digiuni.nl.

Bloomer, M., & Hodkinson, P. (2000). 'Learning careers: Continuity and change in young people's dispositions to learning', *British Journal of Educational Studies*, 26(5), 583–598.

Boud, D. (1999). 'Situating academic development in professional work: Using peer learning', *International Journal for Academic Development*, 4(1), 3–10.

Bourdieu, P. (1984). *Distinction: A social critique of the judgement of taste.* London: Routledge & Kegan Paul.

Brown, J. S., Collins, A., & Duguid, P. (1989). 'Situated cognition and the culture of learning', *Education Researcher*, 18(1), 32–42.

Cox, M., Webb, M., Abbott, C., Blakeley, T., Beauchamps, T., & Rhodes, V. (2004). *A review of the research literature relating to ICT and attainment.* London: Becta.

Drent, M. (2005). *In transitie. Op weg naar innovatief ICT-gebruik op de PABO* [*In transition. On the road to innovative ICT usage at the Pedagogical Academy of Primary Education*]. Enschede: Proefschrift Universiteit Twente. Retrieved 25 May 2007 from www.ictopschool.net/onderzoek.

Engeström, Y. (1994). *Training for change: New approach to instruction and learning in working life.* Geneva: International Labour Office.

Fuller, A., Hodkinson, H., Hodkinson, P., & Unwin, L. (2005). 'Learning as peripheral participation in communities of practice: A reassessment of key concepts in workplace learning', *British Educational Research Journal*, 31(1), 49–68.

Garrick, J. (1998). *Informal learning in the workplace: Unmasking human resource development*. London: Routledge.

Handy, C. (1995). *Trust and the virtual organisation*. Retrieved from http://visionary marketing.com/handytrust.html.

Hezemans, M., & Ritzen, M. (2004). *Communities of practice in de DU. Wat doen we ermee? Samenwerken aan vernieuwing van het Hoger Onderwijs, 403. PUB.059 [Communities of Practice at the Digital University. What are they good for? Collaborating on the innovation paradigm in Higher Education]*. Digitale Universiteit. Retrieved 12 January 2011 from http://www.digiuni.nl.

Hodkinson, H., & Hodkinson, P. (2002). 'Cultures, communities and biographies: Relations between workplace learning and managerialism for schoolteachers'. Paper presented at the SCUTREA Annual Conference, University of Sterling, 2–4 July.

Hodkinson, P., & Hodkinson H. (2003). 'Individuals, communities of practice and the policy context: School teachers' learning in their workplace', *Studies in Continuing Education*, 25(1), 3–21.

Hodkinson, P., Sparkes, A. C., & Hodkinson, H. (1996). *Triumphs and tears: Young people, markets and the transition from school to work*. London: David Fulton.

Jarvenpaa, S. L., & Leidner, D. E. (1998). 'Communication and trust in global virtual teams', *Journal of Computer-Mediated Communications*, 3(4). Retrieved 21 January 2002 from http://www.ascusc.org/jcmc/vol3/issue4/jarvenpaa.html.

Kimble, C., Li, F., & Barlow, A. (2000). 'Effective virtual teams through communities of practice', *Management Science, Theory, Method & Practice*, research paper 2000/9.

Lave, J., & Wenger, E., (1991). *Situated learning: Legitimate peripheral participation*. Cambridge: Cambridge University Press.

McDermott, R. (2001). *Knowing in community: 10 critical success factors in building communities of practice*. Retrieved 25 May 2007 from http://www.co-i-l.com/coil/knowledge-garden/cop/knowing.shtml.

Manville, B., & Foote, N. (1996). *Harvest your worker's knowledge*. Datamination.

Marton, F., Hounsell, D., & Entwistle, N. (eds) (1984). *The experience of learning*. Edinburgh: Scottish Academic Press.

Salomon, G., & Ben-Zvi, D. (2006). 'The difficult marriage between education and technology: Is the marriage doomed?', in L. Verschaffel, F. Dochy, M. Boekaerts and S. Vosniadou (eds), *Instructional Psychology: Past, present, and future trends. (Essays in honour of Erik De Corte)* (pp. 209–222). Amsterdam: Elsevier.

Seely Brown, J., & Duguid, P. (1996). 'Universities in the digital age', *Change*, July/August, 11–19.

Seely Brown, J., & Solomon Gray, E. (1995). *The people are the company*. Retrieved 25 May 2007 from http://www.fastcompany.com/online/01/people.html.

Shaffer, R., & Koehn, D. (2002). *Creating communities of practice – the knowledge bridge builders*. Retrieved 25 May 2007 from http://procop.du.nl/co%C3%B6rdinator.htm.

Slavin, R. (1995). 'Best Evidence synthesis: An intelligent alternative to meta-analysis', *Pergamon, J.Clin Epidemiol*, 48(1), 9–18.

Van den Bossche, P. (2006). *Minds in teams. The influence of social and cognitive factors on team learning*. Maastricht, the Netherlands: Datawyse.

Wenger, E. (1998). *Communities of practice: Learning, meaning and identity*. New York: Cambridge University Press.

Wenger, E., McDermott, R., & Snyder, W. M. (2002). *Cultivating CoPs: A guide to managing knowledge*. Boston, MA: Harvard Business School Press.

Chapter 6

The reflective practitioner: D. Schön

Piet Van den Bossche and Simon Beausaert

Case study: A Personal Development Plan as an assessment tool

In a non-profit governmental organisation 30,000 employees are working in 13 different regions. In this case we will focus on one of those regions where 1,400 employees are located in five different offices in four different cities. While it consists of a very large, bureaucratic organisation, it is described by employees and management as a warm family business because most employees who start working there enjoy the work and are so dedicated to the organisation that they stay there for the rest of their working lives. This has led to an employee average age of 49 years. As a consequence, in a few years the organisation is due to experience the departure of a significant number of experienced workers and, thus, talent management and the continuing professional development of junior staff are high on the strategic agenda. Furthermore, as an effect of computerisation, reorganisations are regularly implemented. This increases the need to take care of the continuing professional development of the employees.

Most employees in the organisation take part in an annual assessment cycle. Formally, the assessment cycle consists of a performance interview, a development interview and an assessment interview with the supervisor. Within the assessment process the supervisor and the employee can make use of two different supporting instruments, namely the 'knowledge-ID' and the 'evaluation form'. While the knowledge-ID provides the supervisor with an extended CV of the employee's previous learning experiences, the evaluation form not only reviews the past year but also looks forward to the future. Together with the supervisor, questions such as 'How does the employee see his or her future?' and 'Does the employee still need to work on certain competences in order to reach his or her goal?' are discussed. Bearing in mind the large stream out that is expected soon, and the reorganisations facing the organisation, the national central HR office decided to implement a new instrument of assessment, namely a Personal Development Plan (PDP). The PDP integrates the knowledge-ID and the evaluation form by outlining the competences the employee still needs to develop (looking forward) through an evaluation of the strengths and weaknesses of the employee (looking back).

In the PDP form the following questions are posed: 'What are your weaknesses?' 'What are your strengths?' 'What do you want to accomplish?' 'Which competences do you still need to develop?' and 'How do you want to develop those competences?' The answers to these questions can be used to inform the dialogue with the supervisor, in which the supervisor will try to stimulate the employee's reflection on the PDP. The dialogue with the supervisor and the employee's reflection are crucial and form the core business of using a PDP. Reflection has several aims. First, by reflecting, the employee should get a better insight into what he or she wants (e.g., promotion, or to keep doing the same job, or learning how to deal with new technologies). Second, by keeping in mind the goal of the employee, reflection should lead towards insights into the employee's strengths and weaknesses that will help or hinder him or her in accomplishing the defined goal. Most employees are not aware of their strengths and weaknesses since they were never encouraged explicitly to think about them, for example during dialogues with colleagues or supervisors. Third, reflection should help the employee to keep track of learning activities undertaken, ranging from undergoing training to looking something up on the Internet, and help to make sure employees think about what was learned during those activities, and how. Most employees only think of learning activities as undertaking training. They are mostly not aware of the fact that they learn everyday, nor of how they do this. Furthermore, to be able to transfer into the job what was learned off the job, follow-up reflection is crucial. The PDP supports the employee in tracking, structuring and thinking about the learning activities undertaken and, consequently, consciously plans future learning activities if necessary. At the end of the process the employee will have worked on his or her professional development and be able to accomplish the set goals.

However, while a small group of employees was very enthusiastic and motivated to use the tool most supervisors and employees perceived doing the interviews and using the tool as a burden. They were very sceptical about the effects of the tool and about the reflection the tool should encourage. The following objections were not uncommon:

> Using a personal development plan leads towards nothing. It is frustrating and not motivating. Against my will I fill in the form every year again. Why are they torturing us with this tool? It's not that I do not know what to do with my time. Besides, my supervisor is not at all occupied with my development.

In other words, many supervisors or employees believed they did not need a tool in order to have good dialogue with their employees or supervisor. It seems as if they think they do not need a PDP in order to talk about their learning and they believe they do not need to be 'forced' to reflect.

Consequently, the tool is not used strictly by every supervisor. Most of the experienced supervisors developed their own way of conducting the interviews and using the instrument. As a result, there exists a lot of variation in how conversations are conducted and how the tools are used, which does not make it a very consistent process for the employees. In addition, many supervisors, especially the younger ones, are not really familiar with the rationale behind the interviews and the forms, nor with how to conduct this kind of conversation.

In summary, while the HR department had high expectations of performance interviews and PDPs some of the employees and supervisors did not really see the advantages. As a consequence, the tool was not properly implemented and used which resulted in perceived ineffectiveness, frustration and window dressing.

In order to tackle these shortcomings a training programme was developed. The training consisted of the following elements. First, the set-up and the underlying goal of the assessment cycle and the tools were explained. Questions like 'Why do we use the formats?' and 'Which standard questions are asked in the format and why?' were discussed. Second, the supervisors were asked to form sub-groups of three to four supervisors and were encouraged to share their experiences of performance interviews and of supporting their employees in using a PDP. Third, a simulation was introduced. In each simulation three supervisors were involved. One of them played the supervisor, one was the employee and the third observed the performance interview. This simulation had different goals. Being the supervisor gives the participant the opportunity to practice. Assuming the role of employee forces the participating supervisor to experience how it feels to undergo a performance interview and discuss your PDP as an employee. Finally, the supervisor who is observing the situation is able to analyse the assessment interview from an objective perspective.

Introduction

For more than thirty years Argyris and Schön have emphasised the need for development in organisations. They believe that not only should organisational members be learning continuously, but so too should the organisation itself. The cooperation between Argyris and Schön has produced an interesting range of ideas on the theory and practice of individual and organisational learning (1978, 1980). Their ideas are presented further in Chapter 8. In addition to his work with Argyris, Schön's own work focuses on the importance of reflection-in-action and had a tremendous influence on educational practices and thinking on professional development.

This chapter, before presenting the main ideas on the reflective practitioner, opened with a case study of a professional development practice used regularly in contemporary organisations. At the end of the chapter we will return to the case study and review it in light of insights taken from Schön's description of the reflective practitioner.

Recognising and educating the reflective practitioner

Donald Schön has influenced considerably our understanding of professional practice and what it entails to become a professional or to educate this professional.

Schön's contribution was to bring 'reflection' into the centre of what professionals do (Smith, 2001). His ideas are developed in two books. The first, *The reflective practitioner*, published in 1983, presents Schön's ideas on the nature of professional knowledge.

The second book, *Educating the reflective practitioner*, published in 1987, questions the kind of professional education that would be appropriate given the uniqueness of professional knowledge as described in the first book. The following sections present some of the core ideas of these books. First, we will describe knowing-in-action, then reflection-in-action and, finally, we will end with the question, 'How do we educate this reflective practitioner?'

Call for a new epistemology of practice: knowing-in-action

The recognition of the reflective practitioner comes from the identification of a new epistemology of practice. This epistemology of practice emerges from the competence and artistry already embedded in skilful practice. This is different from the dominant view, which Schön labels as 'technical rationality', implying that practitioners are instrumental problem-solvers who select technical means that suit particular purposes best. However, the problems a professional is confronted with, argues Schön, do not present themselves as well-formed structures. Often, they are characterised by uncertainty, uniqueness and value conflict.

Schön uses the term 'professional artistry' to describe the intelligent behaviour practitioners display with regard to these situations. This concurs with what Polanyi (1967) termed 'tacit knowledge'. Schön says that the best professionals know more than they can put into words. To manage their challenging work they rely more on the improvisation they have learned in practice or day-to-day activities than on the theory they learned in graduate school. In everyday life we all have specific skills that we use spontaneously. If someone asks how we can ride a bike so easily we usually do not know why. Our knowledge is tacit. We do not think about what we are doing, our knowing is in our action. Professionals at work also recognise a phenomenon, but often cannot give an exact description of it. They depend on tacit knowing-in-action (Schön, 1983).

Schön (1983, 1987) uses the term 'knowing-in-action' to point to the know-how practitioners reveal in their intelligent actions. This knowing is revealed by spontaneous skilful execution. According to Schön, know-how does not consist of rules or plans that we recall from the mind before acting. Skilful action often reveals a 'knowing more than we can say' (Schön, 1983, p. 51). Schön (ibid., p. 54) has stated three main points with regard to knowing:

1   There are actions, recognitions and judgments that professionals do not have to think about during their performance.
2   Professionals do not notice that they learn these things; they just find themselves doing them.

3   Professionals are usually unable to describe the knowing that our action exposes.

In summary, knowing-in-action refers to our mental action. It is publicly observable as a physical performance, like riding a bike. We reveal it through our spontaneous, skilful execution of the performance, and we are typically unable to make it verbally explicit. Our descriptions of knowing-in-action are always constructions, attempts to put into symbolic form what begins by being tacit and spontaneous (Schön, 1987, p. 25).

Reflection-in-action

Next to 'knowing-in-action' Schön talks about 'reflection-in-action'. When trying to maintain our usual patterns of knowing-in-action we may respond to an unexpected happening by dismissing it or by reflecting on it. Much of our reflection depends on how we experience surprise; when something fails to meet our expectations. In contrast, when spontaneous performance produces solely the results we expected, we do not tend to think about it (Schön, 1983, p. 56). Schön discerns two ways of responding by reflection: reflection-on-action and reflection-in-action. To reflect on action means that we review what we have done in order to discover how our knowing-in-action may have contributed to an unexpected outcome. Alternatively, with reflection-in-action we may reflect during the action, without interrupting it, which allows us to adjust what we are doing while we are doing it (Schön, 1987, p. 26). This is sometimes referred to as 'thinking on our feet' (Smith, 2001).

Reflection-in-action and the professional practice

In a further step Schön connects the idea of reflection-in-action to professional practice. First, he defines the meaning of 'practice'. In the first sense the term refers to performance in the scope of professional situations. Second, it also refers to preparation for performance. However, it also includes an element of repetition. According to Schön (1983, p. 60): 'a professional practitioner is a specialist who meets certain kinds of situations again and again'.

Schön argues that professional specialisation can also have negative effects. First, it could narrow the practitioner's vision. Second, when a practice becomes more of a routine and knowing-in-practice becomes increasingly tacit and spontaneous, the practitioner may not notice the opportunities to think about what he is doing. He will follow the same patterns and can become inattentive to phenomena that do not fit the categories of his knowing-in-action. When this happens the practitioner has 'over-learned' what he knows (ibid., p. 61).

Through reflection the practitioner can become aware of and criticise the tacit understandings that have emerged from the experiences of a specialised practice, and he can make new sense of the experience of uncertainty. Reflection-in-action is central to the art through which practitioners sometimes cope with the problematic and differing situations in practice. When the phenomenon does not fit the ordinary categories of knowing-in-practice, the practitioner can criticise or bring to the surface his prime understanding of the phenomenon, construct a new description, and then test the new description in an on-the-spot experiment. Sometimes he can come up with a new theory about the phenomenon. Even if the practitioner finds himself stuck in a problematic situation or dilemma that cannot be changed into a manageable problem he will be able to find a new way of phrasing the problem (ibid., pp. 62–63).

When a practitioner makes sense of a situation that is perceived as unique it is something that is already present in his repertoire. It can be beneficial to see the unfamiliar, unique situation as both similar to and different from the familiar one, even if, at first, it is not possible to say what the reference point is. The familiar situation functions as a preliminary ruling, or a metaphor, or an example for the unfamiliar situation (ibid., p. 68).

When someone reflects in action he becomes a researcher in the practice context. He is not dependent on certain established theory and technique, but he constructs a new theory out of the unique case. According to Schön (ibid., p. 295): 'a reflective practitioner doesn't keep means and ends separately, but defines them interactively as he frames a problematic situation'. In other words, a reflective practitioner does not separate thinking from doing (ibid.).

Moreover, reflection on reflection-in-action may indirectly shape future action. The present reflection on the earlier reflection-in-action begins a dialogue of thinking and doing through which one becomes more skilful (Schön, 1987, p. 31). It may consolidate our new understanding of the problem or invent a more general solution to it.

Educating the reflective practitioner

In looking for educational activities that can help to acquire the above described 'artistry', which is essential to competence, Schön (1987) identifies a range of central characteristics of these educational practices. Fundamental is that one learns by doing. This implies a range of other practices. Instructors need to function more as coaches than as teachers. In the early stages, confusion and mystery reign. The gradual passage to convergence of meaning is mediated by a dialogue of learner and coach. In this dialogue a description of practice is interwoven with performance. This coaching is, again, an art in itself.

Linking Schön's reflective practitioner and the case study

The assessment practice that is described in the case study incorporates different aspects that are crucial in Schön's ideas on the reflective practitioner.

The new epistemology of practice.   Schön stressed that the knowledge inherent in practice is to be understood as artful doing and fruitful for future learning. The implementation of the Professional Development Plan seems also to start from such an understanding of professional practice. The development is closely linked to what the employees experience during their practice.

Reflection as a crucial element of professional practice.   By implementing the Professional Development Plan the organisation is looking to facilitate, support and/or formalise the informal learning that is going on in the organisation. In this way, the PDP is a tool that wants to stimulate reflection. However, it can be noted that the questions that make up the professional development plan are not directly focused on the experiences. They are directed to reflect upon the learning that is going on, not on trying to stimulate the meaning-making of their practice. However, this is something that is ideally the subject of the dialogue with the supervisor (which is part of the assessment cycle that is implemented in the organisation). The supervisor should try to start a conversation on the experienced practice, indirectly guided by the report in the PDP. In that way, the tool, i.e., the PDP, is only a start, the real power lies in the dialogue.

The dialogue between employee and supervisor mediates the development of the reflective practitioner.   By providing the space for a conversation between the supervisor and the employee the case study builds upon the power of the interaction in building meaning. At the same time it shows that is also hard to implement. The disillusionment that is voiced by the employees (e.g., a lack of interest in the process) can be attributed to the fact that these dialogues are not yet providing what they should. But one can applaud the organisation for the fact that it recognises this, and that it counters it by investing in developing the practice of the coaches.

References

Argyris, C., & Schön, D. (1978). *Organizational learning: A theory of action perspective.* Reading, MA: Addison-Wesley.

Argyris, C., & Schön, D. (1980). *Theory in practice: Increasing professional effectiveness* (6th edn). San Francisco, CA: Jossey-Bass.

Polanyi, M. (1967). *The tacit dimension.* New York: Doubleday.

Schön, D. A. (1983). *The reflective practitioner: How professionals think in action.* London: Temple Smith.

Schön, D. A. (1987). *Educating the reflective practitioner*. San Francisco, CA: Oxford.

Smith, M. K. (2001). 'Donald Schön: Learning, reflection and change', *The encyclopedia of informal education*. Retrieved 2 March 2011 from http://www.infed.org/thinkers/et-schon.htm.

Chapter 7

Systems thinking and building learning organisations: P. Senge

Filip Dochy, Jan Laurijssen and Eva Kyndt

Case study: developing a strategic learning and development plan at Kluwer Belgium

Wolters Kluwer is 'The Professional's First Choice' for information, tools and solutions to help deliver quality results more efficiently. Their customer promise is to be the preferred global provider of information-enabled solutions to help professionals manage processes and drive results effectively. They ensure that their customers have the solutions they need, when they need them and in the media best suited to their requirements.

The 2010–2012 strategy for Maximising Value for Customers (see Figure 7.1) centres on being the preferred global provider of intelligent information-enabled solutions that reduce complexity and drive efficiencies for professionals. The company will maximise value for customers by delivering on three strategic priorities: (1) deliver value at the point of use; (2) expand solutions across processes, customers and networks; and (3) raise innovation and effectiveness through global capabilities.

Table 7.1 Wolters Kluwer company information

Revenues	€3.425 billion (2009)
Employees	Approximately 19,300 worldwide
Markets	Legal, Business, Tax, Accounting, Finance, Audit, Risk, Compliance and Healthcare
Operations	Over 40 countries across Europe, North America, Asia Pacific and Latin America
Headquarters	Alphen aan den Rijn, the Netherlands
Stock listing	Euronext Amsterdam: WLSNC.AS, stock code 39590, ISIN code NL0000395903; included in the AEX and Euronext 100 indices

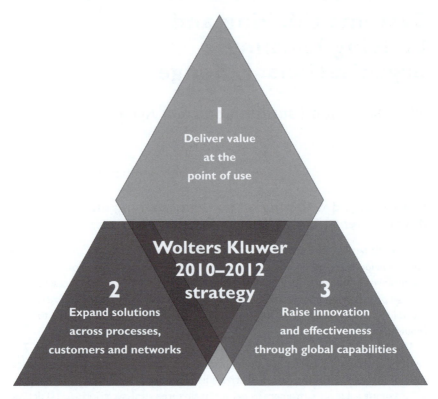

Figure 7.1 Wolters Kluwer strategy

Kluwer Belgium is a market leader in professional know-how and high quality publications, software and services for professionals. They provide information through different information channels and tools that meet customers' needs, such as software, workflow tools, databases and search engines, newsletters, magazines, manuals and training.

To achieve its goals and sustain a competitive advantage in the rapidly changing business environment for information-enabled solutions the company cannot depend upon differences in products and services alone. A great potential for success resides in a highly skilled and motivated workforce that rapidly adapts to changing market conditions. Strategic learning and development can create a performance improvement that enables Kluwer to exceed expectations, and drive sustainable, profitable growth.

Traditionally, the purpose of training and development has been to ensure that employees can effectively accomplish their jobs. Today, the business environment has changed, with intense pressure to stay ahead of the competition through innovation and reinvention (Hooghe, 2008). Convinced of the opportunity, Kluwer's HR Director, Conny Hooghe, was challenged to develop a strategic learning and development plan to support the business development plan.

Clearly, in a highly competitive global marketplace, strategic training and development is key.

(Ibid., p. 1)

What's the plan?

Kluwer developed a strategic plan for training and development that was as top-down as it was bottom-up. 'When strategically applied, continuous learning fosters knowledge and skills acquisition to help the organisation achieve its goals. HR's role is to establish and implement a high-level roadmap for strategic training and development' (ibid.). Or as Kessels (2007, p. 140) puts it: 'a systematic and consistent training policy begins with an analysis of the strategic goals of the organisation and with an analysis of the current work situations within the organisation'.[1] This requires commitment from top management, efforts from middle management and input from all employees.

Kluwer developed a pragmatic project plan in several stages to get a grip on the challenge and deliver in time.

Stage 1: business alignment

In a research paper entitled 'The high impact learning organization: WhatWorks® in the management, governance and operations of modern corporate training', Bersin (2008) listed a number of important topics for training and development professionals. In pole position was business alignment. Understanding the business you are in, the challenges, the competitive environment, the business development plan for the next couple of years, is a prerequisite. Kluwer began by studying the strategic plan for the coming years and discussing it with two members of the senior management team in order to fully understand what the company was aiming for.

Stage 2: expected impact of the strategy on the business

In a second step Kluwer organised, in collaboration with the HR business partners, several workshops with the management teams of each business and supporting unit. Each of these workshops was guided by an identical scenario. The manager in charge was asked to give some highlights on the strategic plan of the company and this was translated and embedded in their own (unit) plan. Second, the participants were asked to reflect and (gu)estimate the impact this would have on the amount and type of work over the next three years.

Stage 3: competences and talents needed to cope

Once the above was identified (and discussed), Kluwer moved on to the next question: What competences, knowledge, skills and talents do you need in order to be able to cope with all the work? As expected, many participants turned to technical skills and knowledge. This provided an opportunity for the facilitator (HR business partner) to confront once again the challenges ahead and what would be required exactly in terms of, for example, behavioural competences, company values, individual talents and so on.

Stage 4: check with people and teams

In this fourth stage, managers were asked to evaluate each team member individually in terms of their strategic competences and to discuss with them what their learning needs and styles were.

Stage 5: consolidate

After analysing the data, Kluwer needed to get the managers back together to consolidate what was needed over the next couple of years. The result of this stage was not just a training plan. After stage 5, a thorough review was compiled on, for example:

- what was needed, and when;
- how the training or learning should be organised;
- who was responsible for what.

Stage 6: plan and communicate

In this stage they communicated clearly to all involved what the result of the exercise was, what to expect from the implementation and they reinforced the building of a shared vision.

Introduction

This chapter focuses on the relevance of learning to the development of business and organisations. It stresses the need for the training and retraining of company personnel in line with the trends of modern business demands. Therefore, we intend to explore the impacts of continuous learning on the development of skills necessary to improve the performance of those engaged in the service of business enterprises. Such training programmes are, without exception, important regardless of status or rank within an organisation.

In making his analysis, Peter Senge uses five basic steps, which he refers to as 'building blocks' that form the basic resource. His five principles or training blocks consist of:

- systems thinking
- personal mastery
- mental models
- building shared vision
- team learning.

It is his aspiration that the adoption and application of these five principles will assist managers, training consultants and personnel to develop competitive business skills as well as healthy intellectual minds, necessary for the growth of business organisations. By adopting these well-tested principles, Senge suggests that organisations grow more quickly, allowing working and management skills to improve rapidly.

It is Senge's belief that the application of these principles and learning skills allows for the creation of teamwork within the organisation. They create a motivating environment for team learning, individual growth, as well as business growth. In addition, the application of these principles opens up avenues for creating a competitive edge in the business world. Also, companies and business organisations develop the empowerment to forecast future business positions, and prepare early enough for difficulties.

Senge's laws

Almost half of new companies will fail within the first five years of their existence, according to Senge: 'Only four [out of ten] of these companies will make it to ten years, and a mere three [out of ten] will make it to fifteen years in business' (Senge, 1990a, p. 117). Senge claims that whenever a company goes sour people are quick to blame a specific problem, and never even give thought to the possibility that it might be a general system problem.

The laws of *The fifth discipline* as put forth by Senge (ibid.) have changed insights into the way learning organisations operate. He calls his core strategy 'systems thinking' (referred to as the 'fifth discipline') which can be described as a different way of thinking in which all employees leave behind their commonly used ways of thinking and start afresh using an 'open-minded way of thought'. At first, this organisational learning strategy will call for additional efforts that finally will lead to a bigger pay-off. In the following four subsections, an explanation will be offered that supports this approach and arguments will be provided to underpin this strategy as a profitable endeavour. Many of the ideas discussed might sound redundant, but they do allow a strong connection to be seen among all the different areas.

The laws of the fifth discipline

Senge (ibid.) points out that in many instances companies are too quick to erase an entire programme because of its lack of overall effectiveness. In too many instances, companies opt to reinvent the wheel rather than look back to see the history of the problem and to increase efforts working out solutions to problems at hand. Senge explains that the turnover rate of employees in companies is so high that it makes it almost impossible to keep a detailed record of a company's past issues, and, thus, newcomers are likely to make the same mistakes as those who left before them. 'Today's problems come from yesterday's solutions' is a first principle that Senge highlights (ibid., p. 2).

Another issue presented in Senge's *The fifth discipline* deals with allowing enough time to pass in order for results to be seen. Especially in this era of a highly demanding market economy where companies want to see results quickly, if there is a problem, they want the 'quick fix', to bring stability back so that no clients or customers are lost, nor do they fall behind their competitors. Senge labels these methods as compensating feedback. He argues against using quick fixes, and suggests looking at the larger picture in order to increase long-term effectiveness.

Senge (ibid.) gives the example of a company whose product is beginning to drop in sales. They react by reducing the price and increasing the advertising. This may work for a short while, but in the long run this band-aid can break and the company then falls back to the previous level or encounters the same problem (evolved into a worse problem) and will spend more to try and solve it again. As mentioned above, when turnover rates are high there is a higher probability that a new employee will have to solve the same problem that was previously tackled by someone else in the organisation. Another reason for people to go for the quick fix is having hidden motives for their actions. Senge gives examples such as fulfilling a quota to get a raise and/or a promotion, or to score points with the boss. The main idea he wants to highlight here is the mentality of the well-known belief that 'patience is a virtue'.

Senge argues for allowing more time to let an innovation take effect. As a consequence, the gain will be much greater and highly appreciated by all (ibid.). Time is the key word here. As Senge asserts, 'cause and effect are not closely related in time and space' (ibid., p. 63). The effect he is referring to are the apparent signs that point out the dilemma.

Senge (ibid.) also points out how these common company solutions are used over and over again in different scenarios, and overwhelmingly lead to a failure in the long run. According to Senge 'the cure can be worse than the disease' (ibid., p. 61) and such resolutions can be 'addictive and dangerous'. The explanation given for this claim is that the dependency on the quick fix makes people too comfortable and they become more inclined never to tackle the real problem. An example in a business situation is the case where the company brings in a consultant in order to 'shift the burden' on to someone else who in turn becomes the lathe of the business. Senge's (ibid.) reference to the shifting-the-burden strategy goes along with the metaphor of putting another band-aid on top of a worn one. Frequent use of the consultant may never lead to a situation where the business is able to be fully functional on its own. Senge suggests that any lasting solution a company does implement needs to 'strengthen the ability of the system to shoulder its own burdens' (ibid., p. 62).

Senge (ibid.) also discusses what he calls 'up front costs'. An organisation must be willing to invest in making some fundamental changes that will benefit the overall well-being of the company and the engagement of employees. For example, training employees in new competencies that facilitate their job; or changes such as making it possible for everyone in the company to be involved with one another in teams: training in teamwork and team learning skills and allowing networking within and among different units, or even company boundary crossing. Many companies do not dare to go this far due to their black-and-white way of seeing the world. A will fix B and nothing else. In order to fix D, C will have to be carried out. No thought is given to E (a general improvement) that could fix B and D, and even F. Connected to the boundary-crossing principle, Senge makes a last point that deals with 'being able to see the big picture'. It involves having contact (not only for the manager, but for all colleagues) with all members of the company. This allows them to see how others view the problem, and how the problem affects them, and not just those in their unit or area. Senge refers to the principle of systems boundary to explain this argument further. It says, 'Interactions that must be examined are those most important to the issue at hand, regardless of parochial organisational boundaries' (ibid., p. 66).

The systems thinking strategy eliminates blaming others for your mistakes. It suggests not wasting energy on pointing the finger and instead suggests using this wasted energy to solve the problem collectively. Senge states: 'the cure lies in the relationship with the enemy' (ibid., p. 67). In many of today's organisations such a strategy is problematic since they do not allow for contact among different units or sectors. This traditional way of working holds that each unit knows best, and collective brainstorming or learning in teams is a waste of time and energy. Including all or most employees in the change process not only eliminates exclusion, but also allows for everyone to have a voice and feel competent. This in turn leads to increased employee satisfaction and a more solid grounding of change and innovation.

The principle of leverage

Senge argues for adapting the principle of leverage. Leverage operates under the principle of 'less is more'. He explains that 'tackling a difficult problem is often a matter of seeing where the high leverage lies . . . A change which with a minimum effort would lead to lasting, significant improvement' (ibid., p. 64). Senge points out that this is more difficult to accomplish than the quick fixes, but methods can be followed to improve the chances of arriving at a highly effective solution. He claims that the foundation of the systems thinking strategy rests on the idea of leverage: 'seeing where actions and changes in structures can lead to significant, enduring improvements' (ibid., p. 114). Traditionally, organisations are not used to acting in such a systematic way. This explains why many organisations are blind to the idea of solving the key problem as opposed to the typical 'low leverage' surface problems. The main idea behind this leverage comes from the principle of economy of means where 'the best results do not come from large scale efforts, but from small, well-focused actions' (ibid.).

A shift of mind

The next subject Senge discusses is that of giving an explanation for what this systems thinking approach really means. He says it is 'a discipline for seeing wholes . . . a framework for seeing interrelationships rather than things, for seeing patterns of change rather than static snapshots' (ibid., p. 68). The systems thinking theory looks at the less obvious structures that are commonly overlooked by companies: 'For the first time in history, humankind has the capacity to create more information than anyone can absorb, to foster far greater interdependency than anyone can manage, and to accelerate change' (ibid., p. 69). This quote puts forth an even greater argument as to why systems thinking is necessary. As Senge argues, it is all about a shift from seeing pieces of the company to seeing it as a company wherein each member makes his or her own contribution, without which the organisation would not work. It is about acknowledging the feedback mechanism which displays how events can complement each other, and vice versa. Moreover, feedback can allow companies to recognise the pattern of structuring mistakes they might be making over and over again. Senge asserts that the ultimate end result to this in-depth process is that a common language is created, enabling the discussion about practices to be more productive as a result of a better understanding of what others are saying.

Senge goes on to elaborate on this topic of creating a common language that produces a chain of circles among the team. Different circles represent different multidirectional cause and effect actions. He points out the significance of these connections among the circles and why it is important to be aware of all the influences. He warns about 'the action of anthropocentrism wherein individuals view themselves as the middle of all the action' (ibid., p. 78). Here also, the feedback mechanism plays an important role. Feedback allows individuals to look at the bigger picture and to see how each person interacts with one another and how each action influences another. This possibly changes preconceived notions they may wrongly have about certain ideas or people. The bottom line in systems thinking is that one suspends his or her idea of there being one individual cause for a specific problem. Senge articulates two different kinds of feedback. First, there is reinforcing feedback 'that exists in a situation where there is an enlargement of any kind at work' (ibid., p. 79). Second, there is balancing feedback that occurs in equilibrating situations where a desired goal is in sight. He is careful to point out that 'delays' are often present in many of these instances and that such disturbances will impede the length of time after which results will be seen. Such delays play a vital role in the creation of a company specific systems thinking method.

Once everyone is able to see how the system actually works, it is possible to understand the influences it had on each part of the organisation (ibid.). A balancing system must then be put into practice where the balancing feedback mechanism (the second fundamental mechanism of the systems thinking paradigm) plays a larger role. Senge equates this process with the scientific concept of homeostasis. It is evident that the system itself is going to carry its own agenda that will affect the actions of the members involved. Planning is a technique for harmonising the balancing system that will generate long-standing goals. Senge highlights how these balancing routines can be more complex than the reinforcing routines due to how difficult they are to detect. A common example of a problem with balance occurs 'when leaders want to alter the organisation's make-up' (ibid., p. 88). Senge claims that this can create 'resistance to change' among colleagues since the leaders are proposing to modify the already accepted norms of the organisation: 'One of the highest leverage points for improving systems per-formance is the minimization of system delays' (Ray Stata, CEO of Analog Devices, in ibid., p. 89).

Delays are a common occurrence in learning organisations and are caused by various reasons (ibid.). As previously mentioned, many feedback loops always include some delaying factor. Types of delays highlighted by Senge are, for example, when an organisation hires a person who has to be trained before being able to work, or if a project is invested in and profit is not seen immediately. When these delays occur, Senge suggests that it is important to allow for a period of time to pass in order for the original goals to be reached. If ample time is not given, something too drastic may be done to correct the error. Senge refers to this phenomenon as 'overshooting' and claims that the more extreme one's behaviour is, the more likely it is that a very different outcome will occur, possibly even the exact opposite of what one wanted to do. Senge also carefully points out that if these delays go unnoticed, attempts to fix them will be even more difficult. The systems thinking perspective is mostly geared towards the long-term outlook, thus supporting the argument of why these delays and feedback loops hold such value.

Templates: identifying the patterns that control events

Two systems archetypes of the systems thinking paradigm will be discussed in this section of the chapter. The first one as stated by Senge is 'the limits to growth', which is 'an augmenting procedure done to come up with a favoured outcome' (ibid., p. 93). It creates a series of desired effects and several consequential effects that 'delay' the desired outcome, and, as mentioned earlier, 'have to be sorted out in the balancing process' (ibid.). Senge asserts that the main management principle here is, 'don't push growth, remove the factors limiting growth' (ibid.). These limits to growth are prevalent in every level of any organisation. Senge suggests that the general path of these limits to growth disturbs organisational transformations and is made to appear successful at first, but then the effects decrease. This possibly forces even more changes that eventually end up in chaos.

The solution to this is certainly not to use actions that proved to be successful in the past, nor to work harder to compensate for the lack of growth. According to Senge (ibid.), the way to achieve 'leverage' in this 'limit to growth' situation is to find and alter the 'limiting factor'. This may mean restructuring the control tower wherein managers redistribute their workload and give some control to the

other employees. Senge says this process is difficult to achieve due to the precon-
ceptions of a manager who is not aware of the competences of his employees to
handle such situations. He also points out that it is important to keep in mind that
limits are ever present, and once one limit has been repaired another one is likely
to surface. It is suggested that the best method for dealing with these limits is to
make and keep track of an organisation-specific diagram of the situation.

The second archetype as put forth by Senge is that of 'shifting the burden'. This
archetype occurs when a difficulty arises and the people who have to deal with the
situation are overwhelmed with its complexity. Instead of finding the root of the
problem they make a quick fix. The main management principle in dealing with
this archetype is 'to be aware of the answer that only addresses the symptoms of
the problem, and not the actual core' (ibid., p. 104). This archetype commonly
appears when the symptoms of a problem appear to be very obvious alongside a
well-known solution, but they still keep a residue of uncertainty. The classic
example of this archetype in companies is when managers bring in an HR
specialist/consultant to deal with a problem. The specific problem may get fixed
by the outsider, but this does not teach the individual manager how to deal with
similar problems in the future. As seen in this example, a 'reinforcing cycle' is at
work within the shifting-the-burden strategy.

The answer as put forth by Senge is to increase independency on the part of the
manager (or whoever needs to address the problem). It is also important to be
honest about quick-fix solutions that are overly used to resolve situations that
will most likely need renewed attention in the future. A 'shared vision' must be
incorporated into the company's mentality. This can be achieved by having
managers who are 'people-oriented' (see also Burke, Stagl, Goodwin, Salas, &
Halpin, 2006). This creates an open-minded environment wherein all employees
have a say and big issues are more likely to be tackled, leading to a shared vision.

Senge (ibid.) claims that these two archetypes are core elements in systems
thinking, and allow organisations to better handle future complications. These
archetypes allow the people involved to recognise and be aware of the common
arenas of the daily work environment, and to think and respond in a more
systematic way. Senge believes these archetypes are particularly useful in the current
high-stress society.

There is also another archetype, though rarely seen, that has a huge impact if
present. Senge refers to it as 'growth and underinvestment': 'building less capacity
than is really needed to serve rising customer demand . . . can recognise growth
and underinvestment by the failure of a firm to achieve its potential growth despite
everyone's tremendously hard work' (ibid., p. 124). A clear sign is when a company
is experiencing financial difficulties which are both a cause and an outcome of
underinvestment and which lead to 'erratic decision making and instability' (ibid.).
Senge also points out how this is usually a never-ending cycle that is almost
religiously followed. One of the reasons many companies experience financial
difficulties is because of previous underinvestment. As shown here, this archetype
can have significant repercussions on a business.

Conclusion

Senge is careful to point out that his goal in systems thinking is that one must systematise the difficulties in order to be able to understand them more clearly. Leverage must be used in order to achieve as much equilibrium as possible. Senge realises that it is very easy to get caught up in the details of a company and ignore its overall mission. He suggests that from time to time it is necessary to step back and look at the whole picture. He believes the ultimate achievement is 'the mastery of the detailed complexity' (ibid., p. 130). When one achieves this it leads towards a 'fundamental solution'.

Building blocks for learning organisations

Learning is an essential, natural process which necessarily forms a vital part of the human world and growth. For an infant it is just as natural as breathing. We do not need to teach an infant how to acquire the techniques of breathing in order to stay alive and healthy. Through the art of learning, children acquire the ability of language acquisition, based on which they are able to speak, starting with their own mother tongues. With the same intrinsic dispositions they begin to take their first walking steps in life, and begin to see the world from the rays of their own lenses.

That children develop and learn certain skills naturally is quite unlike the business world of this modern era whereby consistent learning takes a very central position. In order to keep afloat, maximise results, expand networks and become a successful people manager instead of a perpetual follower, one needs to learn continuously through life. Through learning, one's business knowledge expands: business ideas grow and new techniques evolve. Moreover, learning provides opportunities for employees, managers and CEOs to grow simultaneously, instead of relying on the 'single-source wealth of knowledge emerging and dictated by such an organisation's Bill Gates, Ford, Sloan, or Watson' (ibid., pp. 3–4). It was in line with this reasoning that Senge claimed that the business world in the 1990s had metamorphosed into 'something called a learning organisation'.

It is Senge's considered opinion, therefore, that to have a successful business in the future, business activities have to be genuinely businesslike whereby constant learning skills have to be promoted. Consequently, lifelong learning becomes a key issue and a crucial weapon in the fast developing society. Business has to be pursued as an ever-moving system that is never redundant but, rather, predictable and based on past successes. Senge contends that constant learning enables one to learn faster and in the process sail ahead of other competitors. Through learning, effective and futuristic planning and business forecasts are planted. Above all, 'learning offers the opportunity of getting in line with modern business networks while recognising the complexity and dynamic nature of today's business world' (ibid., p. 4). Through this contention, it is the suggested ideal that the promotion of a successful business activity demands a lot of teamwork, whereby a group of people function together in an extraordinary way, trusting one another as well as complementing the uniqueness of each other's strengths and weaknesses (known as the development of transactive memory systems in teams or other shared mental models). Using the principles of teamwork such as co-construction and constructive conflict (Decuyper, Dochy, & Van den Bossche, 2010) it would be possible to harness together different potential and in the long run enable the building of a healthy and business-minded organisation. The core idea currently is to conceive organisations as business communities where people learn together and develop team learning behaviour (ibid.). By this principle, both managers and employees would see themselves as major stakeholders and co-owners in the venture, instead of perceiving the enterprise as something belonging solely to the CEO of the company. All become part of the enterprise and subsequently contribute to its growth, through the course of the various learning exercises organised by the organisation.

In this section, the intention is to discuss the five building blocks or disciplines proposed by Senge that contribute to the establishment of a healthy and successful business learning organisation. At the root of these building blocks is the need to maintain a business lead, produce extraordinary results and be able to beat all other business competitors by a considerable margin.

The key questions which this part of the chapter intends to address will include the following: What are the basic 'competent technologies' which enable the establishment of healthy business learning organisations? To what extent can these 'competent technologies' contribute to the growth of today's business world?

To answer these questions, an extensive discussion of the five disciplines will be presented. As proposed by Senge, an outline is given for successful business learning environments through his various publications on this subject. These sources shall provide the main data needed for an understanding of this discussion. Also, the opinions of other authors and sources on this essential business topic will be taken into consideration. Support will be given to Senge's mission statement, which was also corroborated by *Fortune* Magazine, which says: 'forget your old, tired ideas about leadership. The most successful corporation of the 1990s will be something called a learning organisation.' With this statement in mind, it only needs to be emphasised that 'superior performance depends on superior learning'. Above all, 'people are born, with intrinsic motivation, self-esteem, dignity, curiosity to learn, joy in learning'.

This highlights the fact that in today's world, business organisations that excel are those which tap into the most creative and innovative resources of their workers and partners, encouraged through consistent learning, at every level of the organisation (Senge, 1990b, p. 1). Edmondson and Moingeon supported this position very positively with the following claim:

> To remain viable in an environment characterised by uncertainty and change, organisations and individuals alike depend upon an ability to learn. Yesterday's

knowledge and skills are vulnerable to obsolescence, and future success requires flexibility, responsiveness and new capabilities.

(Edmondson & Moingeon, 2004, p. 21)

In these claims, the essence of learning is re-emphasised more significantly, while the concept of continuous learning is conceived of as a natural instinct in all human beings. Since this chapter is merely a summation of an extensive strategy, it is not possible to include everything in this discussion.

Senge's five disciplines towards building powerful learning organisations

Engineers say that a new idea has been 'invented' when it is proven to work in the laboratory. The idea becomes an 'innovation' only when it can be replicated reliably on a meaningful scale at practical costs. If the idea is sufficiently important . . . it is called a 'basic innovation', and it creates a new industry or transforms an existing industry. In these terms, learning organisations have been invented, but they have not yet been innovated.

(Senge, 1990a, pp. 5–6)

In the above statement, the author's emphasis on the need for continuing learning within the business organisation is not in any doubt. His assessment of learning, as a key prerogative to a successful business activity, necessary to keep up with the trends of innovation associated with today's business world, is significant.

For Senge, then, to develop a business idea is one thing, but the ability to develop it further into an innovation, through a process of continuous laboratory engineering and learning, becomes very important. It is his belief that all such innovations, reinforced through learning, training and retraining programmes, hold the key to beating all business odds, and competitors. They also keep both employers and employees better informed about the windfalls associated with teamwork, in any organisation. Based on these principles, Senge proposed the steps discussed below, which we categorise here as building blocks, necessary for building successful business learning organisations. According to him, they are the 'five new component technologies' intended to innovate learning organisations:

- systems thinking
- personal mastery
- mental models
- building shared vision
- team learning.

Systems thinking

In today's modern world, the success and survival of any organisation requires some systematic, serious and broad-minded forecasting. Both employer and employees need to plan ahead, think fast and think ahead of time. Such persons need to become very skilled at forecasting, in order to be able to look beyond the immediate business situations. As already pointed out by Senge, a successful business venture in this twenty-first century demands that business owners and proprietors train well, in order to be able to read and understand the signs of future business climates. According to Senge, there are five basic approaches that could be adopted in order to attain a successful business thinking technique (ibid., p. 15).

These approaches are as follows:

Seeing interrelationships, not things and processes, not snapshots   Here, Senge recommends that business managers should see their world of business as a thing that is never static at any time. He suggests that with such foresight, business managers would be able to gather knowledge from other related activities that take place outside their specific areas of business. Such knowledge gained from boundary crossing would help them develop some interrelationship between their specific businesses and other areas of life, too, instead of existing in strict business isolation.

Moving beyond blame   Senge suggests that business managers should hold themselves and their poorly designed systems responsible for any failures and problems encountered in the business, instead of looking elsewhere for causes and explanations.

Distinguishing detail complexity from dynamic complexity   Here, Senge highlights the need to understand fully the dynamic complexity associated with business. According to him, this involves a thorough understanding of certain causes and effects in business, as well as their lingering impacts on the future of such a business organisation.

Focusing on areas of high leverage   In this approach, Senge suggests that adequate attention needs to be concentrated on some well-focused actions and business decisions, which could produce significant and enduring improvements. The key factor remains that they be properly managed and directed towards attaining steady progress.

Avoiding symptomatic solutions   Senge suggests that business managers should avoid applying quick and temporary solutions to business problems. Rather, efforts should be focused on developing long-lasting solutions to such problems, instead of looking for shortcut solutions which would have lingering negative effects.

Based on the above, effective systems thinking demands some strength of foresight, acquired through consistent learning and training, to serve as a source of light and to give a sense of direction, well needed to keep one's business afloat at all times (ibid., p. 7). Such skills would provide adequate capabilities necessary to withstand difficult times, enabling one to lead while all others follow. Armed with this body of well-informed business knowledge, it becomes possible to develop and carve out strategies that could be consulted and applied in the future life of the organisation.

Obviously, this requires the introduction of some new tools, and modern systems, which are necessary to enhance the business organisation's performance towards building a healthy and collaborative learning environment. Here, Senge stresses the need for new and modern technology as part of a necessary strategy for withstanding future problems and difficulties that could affect business growth (Senge, 1990b, pp. 1–17). To that end, he outlines seven tools 'to assist business managers identify archetypes' (or one's way of doing business) that operate in their businesses:

Balancing process with delay   Here, Senge cautions against unnecessary delays, generated by fears of business failure. He advises that business managers should not make unnecessary postponements in investing, based on flimsy excuses. He believes that as long as managers know their business well, that should provide them with enough information about when to invest.

Limits to growth   Senge argues that at a certain time in the life of a business there is the possibility that its growth stops, and may even reverse downwards. According to him, such limits could be brought about by resource constraints, as well as some external or internal factors, which could include poor quality or service.

Shifting the burden   Here, Senge feels that business managers often apply short-term solutions to business problems, with the intention of securing imme-diate solutions, which only succeed in carrying the problem into the future. He contends that the more this quick-solution strategy is applied, the more the organisation loses sight of working out long-term solutions, which, in the pro-cess, affects the professional skills of the staff affected by this short-term attitude to problems.

Eroding goals   In this case, Senge believes that business organisations often find it convenient to lower the standards and quality of their services, as a short-term strategy towards remaining in business. In the process, the organisation could lose its fundamental goals of business.

Escalation   Here, Senge highlights the possibility of unhealthy rivalry and com-petition between two or more business rivals, whereby the success of one implies a negative impact on the growth of the other. In the process, each of them embarks on some aggressive response to the other, once their rival organisation gains a step ahead. The intention is to re-establish a foothold over the other. A typical example is the arms race among the Western countries of the world.

Tragedy of the commons In this case, Senge contends that business managers often intensify their use of a commonly available, but limited, resource until severe diminishing returns set in, with its negative impacts on the organisation. He cited the example of a sheep farmer who keeps increasing his stock without making necessary provisions for a wider area of pasture. In this situation, over-grazing of the limited grazing space occurs.

Growth and underinvestment Senge suggests that rapid investment and business growth demand simultaneous investment in human and physical resources too. Without this, the investment would yield poor results, which hampers the growth of the organisation.

Charting strategic dilemmas

As a further step towards helping business managers to solve different business difficulties, Senge presents seven more tools developed by Charles Hampden-Turner. He maintains that these tools would enable business managers to handle their difficulties and dilemmas creatively (ibid., p. 18). They are as follows:

Eliciting the dilemmas Here, Senge recommends the need to identify areas of business which generate dilemmas, with the intention of handling them professionally to avoid their negative impacts, for example, cost as opposed to quality.

Mapping Here, he suggests that managers need to locate opposing values in their businesses as two different axes, which would help determine their status as well as the position of the business organisation.

Processing Here, he proposes the replacement of nouns with present participles, by adding 'ing', as an indicator of progress and growth, for example, 'strength' should be changed to 'strengthening'.

Framing/contextualising In this, the switching of opposite business values is suggested, with the intention of making each structure the context for the other. By this process, it would become difficult for one business value to claim superiority over the other.

Sequencing Here, it is recommended that there is need for managers to think of business in terms of an ongoing process, instead of accepting it as a static affair, thereby referring it to some particular point in time in the past. He argues that investing in long-term technology yields significant long-term benefits, instead of the other way round.

Waving/cycling   The idea holds that there are certain factors which could lead to business values declining at some particular periods, and still improving at other times. The implication is that business values cannot remain static but are subject to change.

Synergising   It is possible to achieve a business breakthrough and improvement in all the various axes of one's business, which is the ultimate goal of all business.

Finally, it is Senge's opinion (ibid., p. 21) that business leaders should develop a learning laboratory, in which the process of learning together could be designed. This is intended to enhance collective intelligence and professional creativity, as well as design and construct effective practice for management teams. Team learning does indeed seem to be a strong predictor of team efficiency (Decuyper, Dochy *et al.*, 2010). Above all, this process offers the opportunity of combining meaningful business issues with meaningful interpersonal dynamics. The process also encourages the development of new learning skills, within which business leaders who could develop business organisations are trained. Thus, the roles, skills and tools that are necessary for business leadership could be learned.

Personal mastery

This learning building strategy was what Senge referred to as 'the learning organisation's spiritual foundation'. His choice of metaphor is based on the fact that the concept of personal mastery captured within this analysis does not imply a total dominance or complete monopoly of the business area. Rather, his understanding of this learning block makes reference to a person's business ability to maximise results and still make room for other enterprises to thrive in the context of some fair competition. It is our contention that a serious commitment to lifelong learning provides the key with which this target is realised, while recognising the fact that personal mastery involves the discipline of continually clarifying and evolving some deeper foresight, through consistent learning, co-construction and constructive conflict, patience and objectivity (Senge, 1990a, p. 7).

Following this analysis, therefore, one is not surprised to learn of the factors behind the consistent and enviable leading role of Bill Gates' Microsoft products in the computer market today. Despite all the stiff opposition and litigation its opponents mount against the continued dominance of its computer softwares, Microsoft and its allied products continue to take the frontal lead. They continue to succeed where others fail. They reap benefits from the failures and losses of others. Their products continue to dominate and command the software market.

Because of its complete mastery of its product areas, Microsoft became the leading computer software company in the computer market today. The company's attachment to continual learning, market research and surveys, gives it an edge over its other competitors, thereby making all Microsoft products household names in the computer world. This is further encouraged by its investment in staff resources, thereby enabling the company to tap into the resources, energy, intelligence and engagement of its workers and research officers (ibid., pp. 140–141). Accordingly, Senge strongly suggests that managers must necessarily redefine their jobs, and avoid 'the old dogma of planning, organising and controlling' the entire business empire all alone, while recognising the fact that personal mastery goes beyond individual competence and skills alone.

Based on these developments, Senge tries to distinguish between personal learning and organisational learning, with the intention of avoiding a clash between personal and professional commitments to learning. For Senge, this distinction is essential so that individual workers experience unhindered growth through the process of organisational learning, which, in the long run, places the business on some stronger foothold of growth (ibid., pp. 8 and 141). The idea is that the growth of the company implies the growth and advancement of individual persons and workers engaged in the project of building a creative and successful business organisation. This implies building learning companies. Creativity and professionalism, which are necessary for improved productivity and professional performance, are attained. In the process, it becomes possible to attain whatever goals we set for ourselves and for our business which lead to corporate excellence, according to O'Brien (in ibid., p. 143).

Thus, through the mastery of skill, total specialisation is encouraged, which at the same time encourages a mastery of other professions as well as a development of a better sense of vision. With a perfect sense of vision, staff resources are maximally harmonised, professionalism is unhindered, and business goals become attainable, while efficiency and competence are promoted (ibid., pp. 152–154). Moreover, this training exposes workers to the ability to be patient and persevering in their attitudes to work. Thus, the benefits possible from exposing workers to a series of training and retraining exercises are boundless, and incalculable, on the side of the business enterprise and the persons involved. Based on these understandings, Kessels suggested that organisational learning encourages the mastery of tasks, and enables employees to acquire new skills for performing their assigned tasks, skills which subsequently contribute to their personal enrichment of work-related knowledge (Kessels, 1993, p. 2). This can be attained through a series of seminars, training programmes, induction exercises and other related on-the-job programmes which promote workers' lifelong learning and knowledge of professional skills (Elkjaer, 2004, p. 78). Through this learning process, workers' awareness and understanding develop more professionally, thereby empowering them to make a 'genuine commitment' to or engagement with their professional careers (Senge, 1990a, pp. 170–171).

Mental models

Mental models as our personal representations of reality through our experiences affect our actions, perceptions and attitudes (ibid., pp. 175–178). According to Senge, this learning principle requires that we 'shape how we act'. He recommends that people should dispose themselves, their professions and job careers to the dictates and control of their mental images. It is his view that individuals should reflect on or look at their inward selves, in order to develop some personal image about their internal dispositions which could facilitate their systems thinking potentials. Such inner pictures of oneself could become a platform from which to understand oneself and the world much better and more objectively.

Upon following this process Senge suggests that people could learn more meaningfully, objectively and constructively. He cites the case of the Royal Dutch Shell oil company, whose adoption and application of this principle of 'mental models' gained them a competitive advantage in the oil industry in the 1970s. Above all, such a view disposes people to the ideas, knowledge and influence of others. Within this context, ideas could be shared and well-known processes such as co-construction and constructive conflict, sharing and acting took place. Knowledge could be exchanged, and creative business innovations could be accomplished which guide the policies of business managers in the direction of 'openness and merit' (ibid., p. 182). This process compels business managers to take decisions that favour the interests of the organisation, instead of basing such policy matters on unnecessary bureaucratic politics.

Based on this principle, Senge argues that better ideas emerge when ideas are shared, especially as we all see the world from our individual mental lenses. This suggests that the sharing of honest ideas lays the foundation to more critical, powerful and objective thinking, which results in clearer views (ibid., p. 185). It was in recognition of this incentive that one can say that 'ideas shared are ideas sharpened', which results in improved performance. Based on this, a common English adage says that two heads are better than one (ibid., p. 191).

All of the above explains the need to explore and tap into the hidden knowledge, potential and talents which every single individual carries in their inner self, with the intention of improving one's skills, especially in the technological era. Alone, every one of us is rich in individual knowledge. Grouped in teams, it becomes possible to move the immovable and to construct ideas that can move mountains. Through consistent learning and sharing, therefore, knowledge gets sharper and becomes shared in mental models. Creativity develops faster, while critical and objective thinking become tools of business ingenuity and professional expertise in today's business world. Thus, Senge, in recognition of the importance of this learning process, concludes that 'systems thinking without mental models is like the DC-3's radial air-cooled engine without wing flag' (ibid., p. 203).

Building shared vision

This is another major building block that Senge considered to be 'a force in people's heart, a force of impressive power' (ibid., p. 206), and a prerequisite to the establishment of a functional and credible learning organisation. According to Senge, 'a vision is shared when you and I have a similar picture and are committed to one another having it, not just to each of us, individually, having it' (ibid.). Within this principle, all the people involved are enabled to develop some shared foresight, focus and energy for learning, as well as 'pictures of the future'. Senge maintains that such a projected vision fosters the genuine commitment of the employees involved towards realising the organisation's set-goals (ibid., pp. 9 and 207).

It is his conviction that through this approach people excel and learn more quickly, because they perceive themselves as people meant for the company's set-goals. They consider themselves to be potential achievers, since this principle changes people's relationship with their company and encourages the spirit of courage among employers. In the process, employers go the extra mile in pursuit of company visions and set-goals. Senge cited the case of Apple Computer, which became an achiever during the mid-1980s, mainly because of the employees' sense of shared vision (ibid., p. 209).

Through the principle of shared vision, company leaders, business proprietors and employers develop a similar business view, and encourage hard work and strategic planning. As such, business leaders are able to forecast their company's visions, and work towards achieving them together as a team of visionaries. To make this feasible, business managers often employ their power of charisma and diplomacy, and co-opt their workforce into 'building shared vision' (ibid., pp. 211–212). This principle also encourages the development of powerful personal visions, which later generates into shared vision.

Therefore, according to Senge, personal visions grow as they are being shared, through dialogue and interactions, out of which new 'dreams' emerge, while more genuine commitment becomes feasible among the members of a business organisation (ibid., pp. 221–225). In the process, it becomes possible for business organisations to picture the future they wish to create, which is normally positive, and intended to inspire more positive visions. According to Senge, this positive-mindedness guided IBM through its breakthroughs in the computer business in the 1960s, leading to the introduction of the System/360 series (ibid., p. 226).

Overall, the fact remains that visions are shared through the process of learning. Through this process, hosted within the premises of a business organisation, such shared visions are better harnessed, studied and researched, and even become more sharply defined and refined, enabling the attainment of specific set-goals. On the basis of this understanding, Senge strongly advised that business leaders should conceive this notion as one which defines 'where we want to be' in the future (Senge, 1990b, p. 4).

Team learning

As a further step towards building a viable learning organisation, there is need for employees to operate as a team, whereby general output is dependent on both individual excellence and teamwork. According to Senge, employees involved in this learning programme are trained to complement each other in their professional careers (Senge, 1990a, pp. 233–234). On the whole, all operate as a single team, and a single learning and working force. According to Senge, the intelligence of one single person can never be equated with that of a team, within which employees' energy is maximised, leading to commonality of purpose, shared vision and understanding. Thus, through close collaboration with one another in teamwork, ideas are better shared and criticised – intellectually. Above all, teamwork creates the possibility to develop extraordinary talents, and highly co-coordinated actions and shared visions (ibid., p. 236). Schein affirmed that team learning facilitates the building of sufficient common ground and mutual trust in one another, as well as opportunities for openness to objective realities (Schein, 1993, p. 42). This is also acknowledged in the research of Decuyper *et al.* (2010).

Through team learning, individuals grow more quickly – intellectually that is – because of the coming together of different and divergent minds and intellects. Individuals learn to deal creatively with the powerful forces opposing productive dialogue and discussion in working teams. According to Senge, this is what Argyris calls 'defensive routines', whereby employees get protection from one another through the process of learning and sharing together (Senge, 1990a, pp. 237–238). Team learning enhances intellectual dialogue, creates better insights into crisis management, and enables the growth of knowledge and creativity among team members. It encourages adequate opportunities for practice in management teams, and enables a free flow of meaningful and deeper knowledge gathering (ibid., p. 245). Argyris suggested that such intellectual activities could be hosted through seminars, workshops and conferences which enable constructive conflicts (Argyris, 1977, p. 7). Senge concludes that this principle forms the 'fundamental learning unit in modern organisations' (Senge, 1990a, p. 10).

Conclusion

In conclusion, citation is given to the introductory note of the *Journal of Educational Research* (1987), which went as follows:

> Education, as a central institution in modern societies, has contributed much to human welfare, including intellectual, social, and economic development, as well as to the enlargement of knowledge and culture. Greater effectiveness and productivity of education can contribute still more to the advancement of nations throughout the world.

This citation reminds us of the centrality of education and its wealth of knowledge to the growth and advancement of the human world. As human beings, education is crucial in our daily activities. It is unavoidable in our professional careers. It even remains vital in our existence as family men and women. As employers and employees, the gains of educational knowledge are huge.

It is not surprising then, that modern employers of labour, company owners and business proprietors hold learning as a fundamental factor for the survival and growth of their business. Through learning, employees' talents and ingenuity are maximally harnessed and effectively channelled towards the growth of the business. In addition, training and development gives people the opportunity to combine their intellectual strength and physical potential towards attaining the objectives and business visions of their organisation.

According to Smith (2003), such objectives would be fully realised if the training and education offered within the workplace was more clearly defined, more collaborative and more innovative. Smith maintains that through these principles, employees' skilfulness and adaptability to modern business techniques and technology, particularly in this highly technological environment, increase (ibid., p. 67). However, much attention needs to be paid to the creation of a conducive learning environment, which would largely facilitate the process of learning, education and training provided to the workforce. Necessary tools essential for this programme must be provided too, while capable hands, which have been adequately trained for this exercise, should be deployed to handle the trainees. Above all, necessary incentives and motivations should be provided to people both during and after the learning programme, in order to encourage them in applying their knowledge in practice in their professional tasks.

Example

Case:　　Hanover
Focus:　 Peter Senge's mental model of organisational learning
Objective: To determine the impact of this learning model on the growth of Hanover

Background information

According to Senge, Hanover as a business organisation was founded in 1852, and managed to exist until 1969 when it became near-bankrupt and was acquired by the State Mutual Company. It had annual premium sales of $1.5 billion, which was just a fraction of the volume of annual sales of an industrial giant like Aetna. Between 1980 and 1990, its rate of turnover has increased to 19 per cent, which then placed it in sixteenth position among the 68 insurance companies studied by Forbes in January 1990.

As early as 1969, Hanover embarked on a long-term project of reviewing the company's operational systems, which it had used for quite some time. To that effect, the company began to work out some strategies that could make work more relevant to human nature. The company then identified a set of values which could be adopted in order to deal with the problem of hierarchy, which was affecting the company's performance. With the adoption of the strategies of openness and merit, Hanover was able to develop its own approach to managing mental models. 'Openness' was conceived as a sort of game-playing that dominated and controlled people's behaviours in face-to-face meetings within the organisation. On the other hand, 'merit' refers to making decisions based on the best interests of the organisation.

In the 1970s, the ideas of Argyris and his colleagues began to provide possible answers to this problem. The concepts, principles and skills of 'action science' began to be considered as possible approaches towards dealing with organisational problems. That led Hanover to organise a three-day management seminar tagged merit, openness and localness. The intention was to expose all Hanover managers to the basic ideas and practices of action science. It was designed to introduce the core values, as well as enable them and put them into practice in the affairs of the organisation. The first task was to make the managers appreciate what it means to practice merit, openness and localness in a learning organisation.

According to Senge, the traditional consideration of 'merit' means doing what the boss wants. 'Openness' means telling the boss what he wants to hear, while 'localness' refers to doing the dirty stuff that the boss does not want to do. Hanover demonstrated serious commitment towards adopting the mental model as its development strategy, and subsequently embarked on developing it more critically. As a result, it organised a second management training session intended to help the company's managers improve their basic thinking skills. This was meant to expose the managers to the limitations of mechanistic thinking.

The problems

It was discovered in the course of the training that the managers could not tackle the demands of handling complex business issues. Rather, their attitude was comparable to 'fixing a flat tyre' which rather complicated the problems.

The second training programme was tagged 'Thinking about Thinking'. The core content of that training was modelled on the basic moral, ethical and managerial practices of Eastern and Western European cultures, which were adopted as being highly relevant, even though both could lead to opposite conclusions. This development created the insight that there is more than one way to look at such complex business issues. It helps to break down the walls between disciplines in the company, and between different ways of thinking. The impact on managers' understanding of mental models was highly profound.

As a consequence, it became obvious that mental models in Western cultures are incomplete and chronically non-systemic, and introduce people to basic principles of system thinking, while emphasising the difference between process thinking and seeing only 'snapshots'. Hence, systems thinking can be seen as an alternative to the pervasive reductionism in Western cultures. That is the pursuit of answers to complex issues.

The results

According to O'Brien, there was a steady improvement in Hanover's profit margin over the years during which its progress was monitored. It performed better than the industrial average, by a margin of three out of five times, from 1970 to 1974; four out of five times from 1975 to 1979; and eight out of ten times from 1980 to 1989. From 1985 to 1989, the company's average return on equity was 19.8 per cent, compared with 15.9 per cent for the property and liability industry. Its sales growth was 21.8 per cent, compared to 15 per cent for the industry.

In Hanover's 1988 annual report, tagged 'the connection between learning and competitiveness', it was confirmed that its commitment to investing in the education of its staff continued to result in huge benefits. Consequently, Hanover developed its own particular approach to building mental models among its staff, starting with the building of skills through training, frequent management bulletins and continuous training programmes. In time, it established a sound foundation for building basic skills in reflection, surfacing and the public examination of mental models. Thus, mental models retrain our natural inclinations, which enable conversations to produce genuine learning skills, rather than the reinforcement of prior traditional operational skills.

Overall conclusion

> A learning organisation is one which facilitates learning and personal development of all its employees, whilst continually transforming itself.
>
> (Beck, 1989, p. 22)

> A learning organisation is one in which learning is a continuous, strategically used process, integrated with and running parallel to work that may yield changes in individual and collectively held perceptions, thinkings, behaviours, attitudes, values, beliefs, mental models, systems, strategies, policies and procedures.
>
> (Watkins & Marsick, 1992, p. 298)

As indicated in the above quotes, a learning organisation is not merely thrown together on a whim. Even at its roots in the late 1980s much attention was put on the complexity of this strategy. The second definition above is more in depth and is a good, thorough explanation of the make-up of a learning organisation. Throughout this chapter an outline has been given on the broader points of what makes up the fifth discipline, a practical strategy that should be implemented into learning organisations according to Senge. Alongside the ideas expressed examples were given in order to assist the understanding of the strategy. As previously mentioned, Microsoft, Royal Dutch Shell and other major corporations serve as good examples for other companies to follow. Senge gives valid statements as to why his fifth discipline strategy works, and at present and in the future this strategy will continue to change the way companies do business. The systems thinking training block clearly receives the most attention from Peter Senge. Not surprisingly, since he believes that systems thinking is the 'fifth discipline' and as such it can be seen as somehow more fundamental, a prerequisite, to the enhancement and implementation of stronger learning organisations.

Back to the strategic learning and development plan at Kluwer Belgium

The case study presented at the beginning of this chapter describes the process of how a strategic learning development plan came about over a period of six months. Afterwards, we made some reflections in terms of Senge's five disciplines of the learning organisation:

- systems thinking
- personal mastery
- mental models
- building shared vision
- team learning.

Looking back, it is comforting to see that we have managed to integrate these disciplines. 'It's vital that the five disciplines develop as an ensemble', says Senge (2006, p. 11). Reflecting on the project, we found that they were developed as an ensemble but not all at the same pace.

Six stages, five disciplines?

Reflecting on our most interesting and effective project to build a strategic learning and development plan, and evaluating our stages in terms of the five disciplines, we came to the conclusion that in stage 1, business alignment, Kluwer aimed at building a shared vision within the senior management. By studying the context in which the business is situated you acknowledge the importance of this context and the fact that the broader circles around the business can impact your individual organisation. This way of thinking is in line with the systems thinking discipline of Senge. This systems thinking discipline is also demonstrated in stage 2. The reflection on the impact of the strategy on the business demonstrated that interrelationships and processes are recognised, dynamic complexity is distinguished and quick fixes and symptomatic solutions are avoided. The latter are all approaches to fulfilling the systems thinking building block. In order to evaluate the impact of the strategy all participants had to obtain personal mastery regarding the strategy and the business. In this stage, both individual excellence and team learning contributed to the output of the stage.

In the third stage, this 'team' reflected on the competences and talents that were needed in order to implement the strategy successfully. At this point it was important that a shared vision was developed that was characterised by looking for leverage and adopting a long-term perspective. This was achieved by not only focusing on technical skills and knowledge, but also by reflecting on company values, behavioural compentences and so on. The goal of stage 4 was personal mastery of the learning needs of the employees. This process can also be considered a form of the balancing feedback mechanism. Discussing the results of the evaluation of the strategic competences in order to determine the learning needs of the employee in question has the potential to minimise resistance, and, hence, delay. Moreover, minimising delay is one of the highest leverage points for an organisation (see p. 95). Stage 5 is actually the fulfilment of Senge's law to allow more time for an innovation to take effect. It is an inherent part of the systems thinking discipline. In the final stage, the goal is yet again to build a shared vision, this time within the entire business. This shared vision is built by communicating clearly what the results of the exercise were and what is expected from the implementation.

A building block we did not address is 'mental models'. This discipline has so far only been the subject of conversation with the HR Director and business partners. It is not altogether surprising that mental models are missing from our project. On the one hand, one could argue that the mental models are partly incorporated in the action that led to building shared vision. However, this is not necessarily so, since an organisation could build a shared vision without making individual mental models explicit. On the other hand, to make individual mental models explicit requires almost a separate activity. When doing this, and when personal ideas are shared, better ideas emerge, since we all view things from our individual mental lenses. This suggests that the sharing of honest ideas lays the

Table 7.2 The six stages and corresponding disciplines

Stages	The 5 disciplines or building blocks
1 Business alignment	Building shared vision Systems thinking
2 Impact on the business	Personal mastery Team learning Systems thinking
3 Competences and talents needed	Building shared vision Team learning
4 Check with people and teams	Team learning Personal mastery
5 Consolidate	Systems thinking
6 Plan and communicate	Building shared vision

foundation to more critical, powerful and objective thinking, which results in clearer views (Senge, 1990a, p. 185). Perhaps we could have benefited from doing this intensively in a creative way.

Note

1   Translation by Jan Laurijssen.

References

Argyris, C. (1977). 'Double-loop learning in organizations', *Harvard Business Review*, 55(5), 115–25.

Beck, M. (1989). 'Learning organizations: How to create them', *Industrial and Commercial Training*, 21(3), 21–28.

Bersin, J. (2008). 'The high impact learning organization: WhatWorks® in the management, governance and operations of modern corporate training'. Oakland, CA: Bersin & Associates.

Burke, C. S., Stagl, K. C., Goodwin, G. F., Salas, E. , & Halpin, S. M. (2006). 'What type of leadership behaviors are functional in teams? A meta-analysis', *The Leadership Quarterly*, 17, 288–307.

Decuyper, S., Dochy, F., & Van den Bossche, P. (2010). 'Grasping the dynamic complexity of team learning: An integrative model for effective team learning in organizations', *Educational Research Review*, 5, 111–133.

Edmondson, A., & Moingeon, B. (2004). 'From organizational learning to the learning organization', in C. Grey & E. Antonacopoulou (eds), *Essential readings in management learning* (pp. 21–36). London, Thousand Oaks, CA, & New Delhi: Sage Publications.

Elkjaer, B. (2004). 'The learning organization. An undelivered promise', in C. Grey & E. Antonacopoulou (eds), *Essential readings in management learning* (pp. 71–87). London, Thousand Oaks, CA, & New Delhi: Sage Publications.

Hooghe, C. (2008). 'Strategic training and development: A gateway to organizational success', *HR Magazine*, March.

Journal of Educational Research (1987). 'Synthesis of educational productivity research', in H. J. Walberg, T. Neville, & E. De Corte (eds), *International Journal of Educational Research*. Oxford, New York, Toronto, Sydney & Frankfurt: Pergamon Press.

Kessels, J. W. M. (1993). *Corporate education. The ambivalent perspective of knowledge productivity*. Leiden: Centre of Education and Instruction.

Kessels, J. W. M. (2007). *Opleidingskunde. Een bedrijfsgerichte benadering van leerprocessen* [Training and development: A corporate oriented approach of learning processes]. Alphen aan den Rijn, the Netherlands: Kluwer.

O'Brien, B. 'Advanced maturity', available from Hannover Insurance, 100 North Parkway, Worcester, MA 01605.

Schein, E. H. (1993). 'On dialogue, culture, and organisational learning', *Organizational Dynamics*, 22, 40–51.

Senge, P. M. (1990a). *The fifth discipline. The art and practice of the learning organization*. New York: Doubleday/Currency.

Senge, P. M. (1990b). 'The leader's new work: Building learning organisations', *Sloan Management Review*, Fall, 7–23.

Senge, P. M (2006). *The fifth discipline: The art and practice of the learning organization* (2nd edn). New York: Doubleday.

Smith, P. J. (2003). 'Workplace learning and flexibility delivery', *Review of Educational Research*, 73(1), 53–88.

Watkins, K. E., & Marsick, V. (1992). 'Towards a theory of informal and incidental learning in organizations', *International Journal of Lifelong Education*, 11(4), 287–300.

Chapter 8

On organisational learning: C. Argyris

David Gijbels and Roel Spaenhoven

Case study: the Alfa Training

In 2001, on the advice of the local Committee for Prevention and Protection in the Workplace (CPBW), chemical company Bayer Antwerp decided to rethink the safety training programme for new employees. This also paved the way for a new way of thinking about autonomy within the organisation. The apparent contradiction between autonomous behaviour and guided behaviour was at the centre of debate between the prevention department, management and the CPBW members.

As a final conclusion, management compared employees to cyclists in traffic with this metaphor: 'We are going to force our cyclist to ride on our bicycle track, but we will certainly not be locking his handlebars!' At any moment, employees must be able to decide for themselves what they will do, in harmony with their environment. A combination of self-guidance and self-regulation should enable them to assess the risks constantly and adapt their behaviour accordingly. Specifically this could mean that the job cannot be done, or that the existing procedure first needs to be amended. This in turn requires social skills such as an assertive attitude and communicative skills. However, employee self-discipline remains the most essential attitude. This is a prerequisite in order to trust that employees, even without constant guidance and control, observe safety regulations in carrying out their jobs.

Obtaining this self-discipline was declared the ultimate goal of the new training project. A new balance had to be found, with a shift to more autonomous behaviour and active employee participation in the prevention policy.

In association with the prevention and training departments a study group was established, made up of experienced employees, which would investigate accidents involving new employees. Several elements would sometimes cause a chain of events, causing the new employee to fall victim to basic 'mistakes' which had been considered 'impossible'.

This chain of events was influenced by the way other employees in the team, their manager and the newcomer all behaved.

The newly designed training allowed the employees to gain practical knowledge in a safe working environment. To this effect, a set simulating a part of the factory was built, which included machines and sounds like the actual factory. After having made an accident analysis, the study group set new goals for the safety training for new employees. It was decided to abandon classic teaching, where the teacher was in a way 'superior' to the students. The central theme of the new concept was for the employees to learn things themselves, rather than be taught. The former teacher would now take on a coaching role. First, a problem is described and then it is explored. Afterwards, the way the problem is handled is outlined in a plan. The planned actions are also performed and afterwards the employee reflects on what went well and what went badly. This forces the employee to think actively about operations he performed subconsciously. Furthermore, the employee is asked to come up with a solution for those parts of the exercise that went wrong. After some time for reflection, peers get the chance to provide the employee with feedback. The coach plays a mediating role in this process with the next cycle, a new problem can be tackled by the employees.

The context

Both in the chemical and in the food industry, most activities carried out in the technical installations are largely bound by legal obligations from safety and environmental legislation and by quality regulations. In addition to this, many large companies enforce an active prevention policy through a prevention department. As a consequence, a vast number of technical and organisational measures are in force, which gives a strong sense of over-regulation. This is of course the result of years of prevention policy. Therefore, employees in the process industry are required to have a high degree of discipline in carrying out their tasks, so they constantly adhere to the regulations. Those tasks are usually described in binding procedures, outlining the work and the required protective gear in great detail.

Nevertheless, when performing their jobs, employees are expected to remain watchful of risks arising from unforeseen circumstances. In reality, however, this is not always how it works. The more experienced employees develop a kind of company blindness, due to the monotonous nature of their routine jobs. Conversely, it is nearly impossible for new employees to assess the risks on various levels correctly. After all, upon their arrival each job has already been extensively thought out and documented in existing procedures. Moreover, during the normal production process unexpected events are relatively few and far between. Installations are becoming more and more reliable, all but eliminating the occurrence of unforeseen maintenance. Because all risks appear to be controlled, people are inclined to think there is no more danger.

This is obviously not the case. Especially for new employees it holds true that, while they tend to have a general knowledge of safety, they have a hard time turning this knowledge into practical expertise on the shop floor. This is precisely why Bayer's training department got the assignment to develop a new safety training scheme.

The theory: the work of Argyris

Together with his co-author, Donald Schön, Chris Argyris was among the first authors who used the term 'organisational learning'. In their perspective, organisational learning involves the detection and correction of error. In the second edition of his book, *On organisational learning* (2001), Argyris begins his preface by saying that

> ... the better organizations are at learning the more likely it is they will be able to detect and correct errors, and to see when they are unable to detect and correct errors. Also, the more effective organizations are at learning the more likely they will be at being innovative or knowing the limits of their innovation.

With this, Argyris distinguishes between two kinds of learning processes: *single-loop learning* and *double-loop learning*. When the act of detection and correction of error permits the organisation to continue its present policies or achieve its present objectives, the process is called single-loop learning. To illustrate this process the authors usually compare it with a thermostat. A thermostat learns to turn the heat on or off when it is too hot, or too cold. If the thermostat were capable of questioning the ideal temperature, it would not only be detecting error, but would also be questioning the underlying policies and goals. This is a more comprehensive enquiry – double-loop learning (Argyris, 1977). 'Unless people acting as agents for organisations and societies are able to learn how to detect and correct double-loop errors, the survival of the society may be in doubt' (Argyris & Schön, 1978, p. 5). Argyris and Schön believe that most organisations do quite well at single-loop learning, but have great difficulties with double-loop learning (ibid., p. 3). One of their main assertions is that organisations even tend to create learning systems that inhibit double-loop learning. Below, we elaborate on the theory of single- and double-loop learning. The work of Donald Schön on the concept of the 'reflective practitioner' is described in Chapter 6.

Theories of action

Argyris (1977) admits that it is not easy to create organisations capable of double-loop learning, but it can be done. A good starting point is to introduce Argyris and Schön's thoughts on the theories of action. People have theories that they use to plan and carry out their actions. Argyris and Schön believe that there are two such theories of action, the *espoused theory* and the *theory-in-use*.

> When someone is asked how he would behave under certain circumstances, the answer he usually gives is his espoused theory of action for that situation. This is his theory of action to which he gives allegiance and which, upon request, he communicates to others. However, the theory that actually governs his actions is his theory-in-use, which may or may not be compatible

with his espoused theory; furthermore, the individual may or may not be aware of the incompatibility of the two theories.

(Argyris & Schön, 1980, p. 8)

Argyris and Schön developed a model of the assumptions they had seen people using and called it Model I. They identified four basic values that govern the behaviour of people who operate by Model I. They are:

1   to define in their own terms the purpose of the situation in which they find themselves;
2   to win;
3   to suppress their own and others' feelings; and
4   to emphasise the intellectual and de-emphasise the emotional aspects of the problems.

The strategy people use to satisfy these governing variables is to unilaterally control the task, the environment and others. The consequences of this behaviour will be single-loop learning, but it will include little public testing of ideas (Argyris, 1977). Also associated with Model I theory-in-use are defensive routines. These are practices that keep the organisational members from experiencing embarrassment or threat. They also prevent the individuals from identifying, reducing and correcting the causes of the embarrassment or threat (Argyris, 1994). Since the actors do not invite confrontation of the inconsistencies within their theories of action, Model I theories of action might be difficult to correct (Argyris, 1977, 2002).

When people operating by Model I try to solve double-loop problems, they will, for example, withhold information that is potentially threatening to themselves or to others, and the act of cover-up itself is closed to discussion. It is highly probable that the other people operating by Model I expect the received information to be inconsistent, vague and ambiguous. Argyris believes that these factors tend to reinforce each other and eventually form a tight system that inhibits individual and organisational learning (ibid.).

Obviously it is preferable for organisational members not to operate according to these learning systems. In order to change these learning systems, people must develop internal assumptions that are different from Model I. Model II is such an alternative. Operating according to Model II can produce double-loop learning in organisations.

> The underlying aims of Model II are to help people to produce valid information, make informed choices, and develop an internal commitment to those choices. Embedded in these values is the assumption that power (for double-loop learning) comes from having reliable information, from being competent, from taking on personnel responsibilities, and from monitoring continually the effectiveness of one's decisions.
>
> (Ibid., p. 116)

As you can see, Argyris and Schön developed two models that describe features of the theories-in-use that either inhibit or enhance double-loop learning. Notice that Model I and Model II are not opposites. Both single- and double-loop learning are essential for organisational fitness (Nutley & Davies, 2001). And 'the capacity for double-loop learning does not inhibit single-loop learning; indeed, it usually helps it' (Argyris, 1977, p. 118).

Organisational theories of action

Does an organisation have theories of action? It is indeed tempting to apply this line of thinking to the problem of understanding organisational learning. Could it be possible that organisations also have theories of action that inform their actions? They would have an espoused theory that they would be expressing to the world. But they would also have a theory-in-use, one that could only be inferred from directly observable behaviour (Argyris & Schön, 1978, p. 11).

Although this path is full of obstacles, Argyris and Schön spell out three conditions to be met in order to talk about an organisation:

1   making decisions in the name of the collective;
2   delegating to individuals the authority to act for the collective; and
3   setting boundaries between the collective and the rest of the world.

When these conditions are met, there can and will be an *organisational 'we'* that can decide and act (ibid., p. 13).

As a next step, criteria can be set up to be met in order to to talk about organisational theory-in-use.

> Organizational theory-in-use is to be inferred from observations of organizational behaviour – that is, from organizational decisions and actions. The decisions and actions carried out by individuals are organizational insofar as they are governed by collective rules for decision and delegation. These alone are the decisions and actions taken in the name of the organization.
>
> (Ibid.)

Images and maps

Every member constructs his own representation of the theory-in-use of the organisation. This image is always incomplete and organisational members strive continually to complete it. But these individual, privately held *images of the theory-in-use* of the organisation cannot account for organisational continuity. After all, in most organisations it is impossible to compare and adjust these images through face-to-face interaction. Therefore, public representations of organisational theory-in-use must be present. These are what Argyris and Schön (ibid., pp. 16–17) call *organisational maps*. Organisational maps are shared descriptions of the organisation, jointly constructed by the individuals. They include, for example, diagrams of the work-flow and compensation charts; even a building can function as a map. These maps not only describe the actual patterns of behaviour, but organisational members also use these maps to guide their own enquiry.

> Organizational theory-in-use, continually constructed through individual inquiry, is encoded in private images and in public maps. These are the media of organizational learning.
>
> (Ibid., p. 17)

Organisational learning

Considering the previous statements, the processes of single- and double-loop learning can be redefined. After all, through the continuous modification of organisational maps and images, organisational members bring about changes in the organisational theory-in-use. However, not all these changes qualify as learning.

One can talk about single-loop learning when '. . . members of the organization respond to changes in the internal and external environments of the organization by detecting errors which they then correct so as to maintain the central features of organizational theory-in-use' (ibid., p. 18). You may have noticed by now that single-loop learning is primarily concerned with effectiveness and routine.

> We will give the name *double-loop learning* to those sorts of organizational inquiry which resolve incompatible organizational norms by setting new priorities and weightings of norms, or by restructuring norms themselves together with associated strategies and assumptions.
>
> (Ibid., p. 24)

However, it must be clear that organisational learning is not the same thing as individual learning, although there is something paradoxical. Organisational learning is not merely individual learning, yet organisations learn only through the experience and actions of individuals. There can be no organisational learning without individual learning. Although individual learning is necessary for organisational learning, it is insufficient (ibid., p. 9).

> In order for organizational learning to occur, learning agents' discoveries, inventions and evaluations must be embedded in organizational memory. They must become encoded in the individual images and the shared maps of organizational theory-in-use from which individual members will subsequently act. If this encoding does not occur, individuals will have learned but the organization will not have done so.
>
> (Ibid., p. 19)

A critical reflection on the Alfa case inspired by Argyris' (and other) theories

Accident analyses within the company show on multiple occasions that employee response does not follow procedure at all, and sometimes stems from an intuitive reaction. The more experienced employee will use his experience and his sound implicit knowledge of circumstances in the company. New employees, however, might make the wrong 'intuitive' decisions, harming the installation, co-workers or themselves in the process. It is at this point that training professionals are challenged to try and remedy this situation. When people end up doing something else in reality than what they had assumed, there is a possibility to influence those assumptions and develop more efficient behaviour. Argyris' ideas fit in well with the developments at Bayer and also help to understand the success of the Alfa Training; from Model I thinking in training to Model I *and* II thinking in training and learning with specific attention to reflecting on the discrepancy between theory-in-use and the espoused theory. Below, we illustrate where we can situate espoused theories, theories-in-use, organisational maps and double-loop organisational learning in the Alfa case.

The already substantial efforts in the field of safety, environmental and quality training did not yield adequate results in young employees' behaviour. At that time, there was already a theoretically sound training, including practical demonstrations to support the theory. There was a clear transfer problem: in the workplace the risks were underestimated and the regulations were not followed or were inaccurately followed.

One of the underlying causes of this was social pressure, arising in a team when a new co-worker would join in and learn the ropes, wanting to conform as quickly as possible to the existing habits within the team. This form of adapting illustrates single-loop learning and the habits illustrate theory-in-use. Those habits are mostly based on sometimes large distances in hierarchy, and also cause a limitation for the newcomer in assertively dealing with risks. Preventive personal protection gear is then used in the wrong way or not at all.

A disappointing result of these social processes was the lack of participation in the active prevention policy, despite an open atmosphere being encouraged during the welcoming programme. Specifically, this meant that new employees did not communicate about risks openly, once they had learned the ropes in the workplace. This is a great illustration of the discrepancy between the espoused theory, which was central in training, and theory-in-use in the reality of the workplace.

Another theme under enquiry was the victims' and colleagues' behaviour when an accident occurred. In training, the goal was made clear to minimise any damage by using company tools such as eye-rinsing bottles, emergency showers and extinguishing agents. Giving first aid and calling and guiding emergency services did not go according to the regulations designed for these kinds of situations either. It was soon obvious that people react differently in an emergency than what they imagine in a controlled (training) environment.

One of the underlying causes is the fact that, when faced with a crisis, people no longer react in a cognitive way. The rush of adrenaline gives the 'fight or flight' reflex the upper hand. This causes behaviour to be driven by intuition rather than by logical factors.

In order to react appropriately in such situations people need to have sufficient self-knowledge based on personal experience. Only then will they be able to train their reflexes somewhat and show autonomous behaviour in complex threatening situations.

This impressive conclusion led to a goal being set for the entire organisation, including its values and attitudes, to undergo a transformation. Besides the practical approach of the training, an 'autonomous' employee was envisaged who would join in the thinking process, take initiatives to minimise damage and who would even want, and be allowed, to play a preventing role in his or her working environment.

The revamped learning programme would comprise a practical training which was to be embedded in the first training period of new employees, with support in the workplace.

The Alfa Training got its name as a symbol for a fresh start, but also from the exemplary behaviour of alpha wolves in a pack. Existing training methods were not delivering adequate results, so a new kind of practical training had to be developed. Given the potentially high risks of training in the real production environment of a chemical company, a simulated environment was built for this training. In a 100-m^2 space chemical processing equipment was installed, including pumps, tanks, stirrers, filters, tubes, flanges and the like. Here, we could safely call the Alfa Training an *organisational map*, as Argyris describes the concept.

This equipment used water (Alfa Acid) and air (Alfa Gas) to imitate the most important hazards that are actively controlled in the chemical industry. This 'safe' learning environment allows for a number of tasks to be performed. All products and components of production are realistically documented and described. The procedures are outlined in manuals available to the trainees.

Starting from several specific situations, realistic technical and organisational errors and mistakes were identified using the *critical incidents method*. These mistakes are built into the simulator and can be activated by the coach. Over the course of several sessions, scenarios are generated in which the participant learns to control a complex, changing environment.

An important aspect is that participants are given the chance to discover through multiple repeats in the safe learning environment how to keep 'improving' their behaviour.

Approximately eight participants form four teams of two. During the exercise, two teams work in the installation, the other two teams observe.

As part of the exercise the supervised teams set about not only performing but also planning their own jobs, something normally done for them by others. While they carry out their tasks the coach introduces realistic problems that cause a series of unforeseen circumstances. In the event of insufficient preventive protection during job preparation and execution, damage is sustained.

After the exercise the participants check whether the result corresponds to what they had planned, and they reflect on how they behaved and why. During an evaluation session the other two teams provide their feedback.

The coach adds some value to this, stemming from his or her experience, giving the participants a sense of what is essential in controlling risks. Openness is at its peak in this exchange, and the resulting learning tension is fully utilised at that moment.

The latter also helps to reinforce the participants' reflective abilities, increasing their self-knowledge and enabling them to act more assertively towards each other and the coach. By talking openly about incidents and adapting their behaviour throughout the training, they work towards increasing their learning ability, and each time they are energised and eager to accumulate new knowledge. Over the course of the five half-day sessions the coach gradually reduces the amount of external control on the learning process.

The participants gain insight into the story of the development of the regulations (risk management in the area of safety, environment and quality). This insight grows together with the complexity of their learning tasks. The resulting way of learning is experienced as pleasant and actually builds substantial intrinsic motivation to 'do well'. This makes participants connect their individual well-being with the goals of the organisation once again. Once you are at that stage you no longer need to explain the value of, say, a procedure in a training session . . . they will actively look for it!

After the training, participants are able to apply regulations in the workplace, constantly assess possible risks, analyse their own working methods critically, justify their behaviour assertively and avoid assuming the role of the passive victim. Statements along the lines of 'it's OK not to be OK', which former Alfa Training participants keep using in the workplace, illustrate how espoused theory and theory-in-use can come closer together.

Embedding Alfa Training into the training programme for new employees is aided by involving first-line managers in the programme. 'Playing' an active coaching role in the exercises allows them to gain insight into a number of aspects of their own leadership, going far beyond what a class or workshop approach would accomplish. The methods are also used to shape training in the workplace. Especially by creating moments of reflection, relationships in the organisation improve in the long term. This helps to support the trust in employees' autonomy. In practice, spontaneous discussions started in several work teams about the consequences of their way of working for new employees. Some teams incorporated the theme systematically in their group discussions. This way, the Alfa training even transcends individual learning and becomes a means to stimulate 'organisational learning' as it was coined by Argyris.

References

Argyris, C. (1977). 'Double-loop learning in organizations', *Harvard Business Review*, 55(5), 115–125.

Argyris, C. (1994). 'Good communication that blocks learning', *Harvard Business Review*, July–August, 77–85.

Argyris, C. (2001). *On organizational learning* (2nd edn). Oxford: Blackwell Business.

Argyris, C. (2002). 'Double-loop learning, teaching, and research', *Academy of Management Learning and Education*, 1(2), 206–218.

Argyris, C., & Schön, D. (1978). *Organizational learning: A theory of action perspective.* Reading, MA: Addison-Wesley.

Argyris, C., & Schön, D. (1980). *Theory in practice: Increasing professional effectiveness* (6th edn). San Francisco, CA: Jossey-Bass.

Nutley, S. M., & Davies, H. T. O. (2001). 'Developing organizational learning in the NHS', *Medical Education*, 35, 35–42.

Chapter 9

Inter-organisational expansive learning at work

Filip Dochy, Yrjö Engeström,
Annalisa Sannino and Niel Van Meeuwen

Case study: 'Tourism for everyone!'

'Tourism for everyone!' is one of the main messages of the Flemish Department of Tourism. And yet, not every family has the financial means to go on a holiday or a day trip. The government's 'Holiday Participation' service addresses itself to these people and offers an attractive option for people on a low income. It does this by:

- cooperating in the development of a social tourism policy;
- looking for tourism partners with a social mindset;
- promoting holidays to people on a low income;
- organising training for social and tourism partners;
- mediating for customised holidays;
- organising evaluation, reflection and exchange to optimise impact; and
- moving into the international context and making contacts.

To make these objectives possible, the 'Holiday Participation' service works a lot with organisations who are willing to offer some of their places to people on low incomes. For these organisations it means that they need to organise themselves a bit differently. People on low incomes are sometimes not highly educated or may be poor readers, so a letter with detailed instructions and juridical information may not be helpful. For a youth camp 150 km from home, transport may have to be organised as many parents on low incomes would not have a car with which to bring their children. For some people it could be the first time they've left their home for any extended period, and this comes with a lot of questions and emotions beforehand, as well as during the holiday. Also, difficult family issues and emotional stress are more likely to occur in impoverished families or those on a low income. Many organisations that offer these opportunities in their programme are working with volunteers who provide guidance at the holiday and youth camps.

The 'Holiday Participation' service was recently faced with many similar questions and challenges from other organisations that offer tourism opportunities for people on a low income. At the same time, there are a lot of good examples within these organisations of dealing with these challenges. In order to optimise the activities of every organisation, the 'Holiday Participation' service initiated a 'learning network' for all interested organisations, each of them with a different background and culture. These organisations were providers of youth camps, family holidays, day trips and so on. They were situated in the youth work sector, the leisure industry, the social sector or were commercial providers of holiday activities. Some of them worked with volunteers, others with employees. Some were non-profit organisations funded by the government, others were self-financing. The point of coming together was to learn from each other's good practices, promote partnerships and create new ways of handling the challenges of working with this target group. This learning network meets around six times a year and works on three main issues.

As a first step, all organisations worked on collaboratively creating a shared vision and meaning about how powerful tourism participation should be and what it should look like. By sharing interest, good practices and stories, we designed a group of shared principles in looking at this niche of the work of the organisations. These shared principles were necessary to value approaches to the different challenges and to discuss and design new solutions out of a shared understanding.

As a second step, the network created thematic workshops or learning days. For these events the network organises discussions and conversations around a specific topic (e.g., generating means; acting upon non-payers; educating volunteers). These thematic sessions are prepared by some of the organisations.

A third step, which we are adopting now, is creating advice for policy makers, through which the network hopes to optimise the practice of holiday participation. In conversations with the policy makers, and even the ministry of tourism, we try to influence the social tourism policy and all participating organisations at the same time.

As well as meeting and learning from each other in real life, the network also meets online on a platform to exchange ideas and documents, and keep each other posted about their activities.

The learning network now consists of more than 40 organisations who attend network activities regularly, both offline and online. It has already resulted in several publications on specific themes, and the ministry of tourism has also adopted the network in its future policy.

Introduction

Cultural-historical activity theory is a framework aimed at transcending the dichotomies of micro-level, macro-level, mental and material activities, and observation and intervention in the analysis and redesign of work and learning. This theory has evolved over three consecutive generations of research. The emerging third generation takes two interacting activity systems as its minimal unit of analysis against which goal-directed actions and more automatic operations are interpreted.

Activity-theoretical ideas have increasing influence on studies of learning and teaching. There is a steady flow of publications that apply activity theory empirically and discuss and formulate ideas related to activity theory. However, activity theory still tends to be understood at a relatively superficial level. Engeström and Miettinen (1999) and more recently Roth and Lee (2007) have pointed out that the rich insights of activity theory have largely remained a well-kept secret to the Western scientific community. As activity theory is the basis of the theory of expansive learning, the central focus of this chapter, we will try to unravel the veil of mystery covering activity theory. Nevertheless, we do not try to offer an exhaustive overview. A more complete overview can be found in a recent article published in *Educational Research Review* (Engeström & Sannino, 2010).

Because an activity system is constantly working through contradictions within and between its elements, new qualitative forms of activity emerge as solutions to the contradictions of the preceding form. Such transformations proceed through stepwise cycles of expansive learning. An expansive learning cycle begins with actions of questioning the existing standard practice, then proceeds to actions of analysing its contradictions and modelling a vision for its zone of proximal development, and ends with actions of examining, implementing and consolidating the new model in practice. As such, expansive learning is different from both the acquisition-based and the participation-based approaches that share much of the same conservative bias. 'In expansive learning, learners learn something that is not yet there. In other words, the learners construct a new object and concept for their collective activity, and implement this new object and concept in practice' (ibid., p. 2). This expansion metaphor can thus be seen as a radical alternative and extension of the acquisition and participation metaphors proposed by Sfard (1998).

In this chapter we focus on the interpretation of activity theory developed by researchers at the Center for Research on Activity, Development and Learning (CRADLE) at the University of Helsinki. In several recent studies CRADLE researchers have concentrated on how learning happens in settings of co-configuration work. Because these new forms of work organisation require 'knot-working' across boundaries, expansive learning increasingly involves horizontal widening of collective expertise by means of negotiating, debating, exchanging information and hybridising different perspectives and conceptualisations. These developments make the theory of expansive learning particularly relevant for studies and practical development efforts in inter-organisational learning.

In the next section we will discuss the three generations of cultural-historical activity theory. After that we will elaborate on five core principles of activity theory. These two steps are necessary in order to understand the foundations of the theory of expansive learning, which are explained in the next section. After that we will discuss recent research on new forms of expansive learning at work, specifically on co-configuration. Next, an application of inter-organisational expansive learning in children's medical care will be discussed in order to give an idea of how the theory is used in practical settings. Another example is then presented, based on recent intervention work promoting forms of sustainable agriculture in Africa. Finally, we put forward some concluding remarks about the theory in general and about its applications in real life.

Cultural-historical activity theory as foundation of the theory of expansive learning

Engeström's (1987) theory of expansive learning is based on cultural-historical activity theory, which was initiated in the 1920s and 1930s by a group of revolutionary Russian psychologists. The basic concepts of this approach were formulated by Lev Vygotsky and further developed by A. N. Leont'ev, A. R. Luria and their colleagues and disciples. Building on Karl Marx's legacy, Vygotsky, Leont'ev and Luria constructed a new theory where mediated and object-oriented activity was at the centre of explaining the acts of human life. Today activity theory is a global multidisciplinary research approach. Besides more traditional domains of psychology and education, the study of work, organisations and technologies constitutes an important domain for current activity-theoretical research (Engeström, 2000). When looking at the developmental history of cultural-historical activity theory, three generations of research can be distinguished.

First generation: mediated action

The first generation of research was centred on Vygotsky's ideas and focused on the idea of mediation. Vygotsky's famous triangular model, in which the conditioned direct link between stimulus and response was transcended by a mediating artefact, represents this idea of mediation. This cultural mediation of actions is often presented as the triad of subject, object and mediating artefact (Figure 9.1.). A human individual never reacts directly to environment, inborn reflexes excluded. The relationship between the human agent and the objects is mediated by cultural means, namely tools and signs.

As a result of the insertion of cultural mediators (artefacts) into human action, the basic unit of analysis overcame the dualism that existed between the Cartesian individual and the untouchable societal structure (Engeström, 2001). The individual is no longer an isolated entity, but must be understood in the context of his or her cultural means; and, vice versa, the society should be understood as being constantly reproduced and changed by actions which use and produce artefacts. Objects became cultural entities and the object-orientedness of action

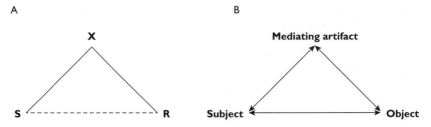

Figure 9.1 Vygotsky's model of mediated action (A) and its common reformulation (B).

became the key to an understanding of the human psyche. However, this first generation of research and theorising remained focused at the individual level. This limitation was overcome by the second generation.

Second generation: collective activity system

The second generation was inspirited by Leont'ev's work. Leont'ev used Marx's concept of labour as a model of human object-oriented activity. Mediated by tools, work is also basically done in situations of collective activity which are characterised by division of labour.

> Only through a relation with other people does man relate to nature itself, which means that labour appears from the very beginning as a process mediated by tools (in the broad sense) and at the same time mediated socially.
>
> (Leont'ev, 1981, p. 208)

The distinction between activity, action and operation became the basis of Leont'ev's three-level model of activity. The bottom level of automatic operations is driven by the tools and conditions of the actions at hand, the middle level of individual or group action is driven by a conscious goal, and the upper level of collective activity is driven by an object-related motive (Leont'ev, 1978). Nevertheless, Leont'ev never expanded Vygotsky's original model graphically into a model of a collective activity system. Figure 9.2 represents such a model.

The uppermost sub-triangle of Figure 9.2 can be seen as the tip of the iceberg in the way that it represents individual and group actions embedded in a collective activity system. Object-oriented actions are always, explicitly or implicitly, characterised by ambiguity, surprise, interpretation, sense making and potential for change.

In Figure 9.2, the subject refers to the individual or sub-group whose point of view is chosen in the analysis. The object refers to the 'raw material' or 'problem space' at which the activity is directed and which is transformed into outcomes

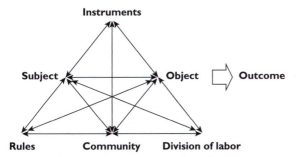

Figure 9.2 The structure of a human activity system (Engeström, 1987, p. 78).

with the help of mediating instruments, including both tools and signs. The community comprises multiple individuals and/or sub-groups who share the same general object and who construct themselves as being distinct from other communities. The division of labour refers to both the horizontal division of tasks between the members of the community and to the vertical division of power and status. Finally, the rules refer to the explicit and implicit regulations, norms and conventions that constrain actions and interactions within the activity system.

The object moves from an initial state of unreflected, situationally given 'raw material' to a collectively meaningful object constructed by the activity system. The object of activity is a moving target, not reducible to conscious short-term goals. Activity cannot be reduced to actions. Actions are relatively short-lived and have a temporally clear-cut beginning and end. Activity systems evolve over lengthy periods of time, often taking the form of institutions and organisations.

The concept of activity took the paradigm a great step forward in that it extended the focus of analysis to encompass the complex interrelations between the individual subject and his or her community. The activity system as a unit of analysis became a powerful conceptual lens on the development and functioning of organisations and collectives.

This second generation of activity theory was initially not sensitive towards cultural diversity. When activity theory went international, questions of diversity and dialogue between different traditions became serious challenges (Engeström, 2001). These challenges must be faced by the third generation.

Third generation: multiple interacting activity systems

The emerging third generation of activity theory needed to develop conceptual tools to understand dialogue, multiple perspectives and voices, and networks of activity systems. The basic model was expanded to include two interacting activity systems as the minimal unit of analysis (see Figure 9.3). In this form, activity theory is also gaining the attention of researchers interested in the challenges and possibilities of inter-organisational learning. The third generation of activity theory will be discussed in detail in the next section.

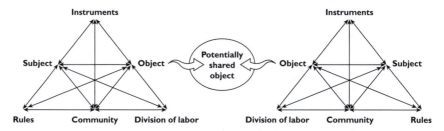

Figure 9.3 Two interacting activity systems as minimal model for the third generation of activity theory.

Five principles of activity theory

In its current phase of development, activity theory may be characterised with the help of five principles (ibid.; for a slightly different formulation, see Engeström, 2005, p. 315).

The first principle is that the prime unit of analysis is a collective activity system, seen in its network relations to other activity systems. Goal-directed individual and group actions, as well as automatic operations, are relatively independent but subordinate units of analysis. Actions and operations can only be understood when interpreted against the background of entire activity systems. Activity systems realise and reproduce themselves by generating actions and operations.

The second principle is the multi-voicedness and the heterogeneity of activity systems. An activity system is always a community of multiple points of view, traditions and interests. Different subjects, due to their different histories and positions in the division of labour, construct the object and the other components of the activity in different, partially overlapping and partially conflicting ways. The activity system itself carries multiple layers and strands of history engraved in its artefacts, rules and conventions. The multi-voicedness is multiplied in networks of interacting activity systems. It is a source of trouble and a source of innovation, demanding actions of translation and negotiation.

The third principle contains the historicity of an activity system. Activity systems take shape and get transformed over lengthy periods of time. Their problems and potentials can only be understood against their own history. History itself needs to be studied as local history of the activity and its objects, and as history of the theoretical ideas and tools that have shaped the activity. Thus, work needs to be analysed against the history of its local organisation and against the more global history of the concepts, procedures and tools employed and accumulated in the local activity.

The fourth principle is the central role of contradictions as sources of change and development. Contradictions are not the same as problems or conflicts. Contradictions are historically accumulating structural tensions within and between activity systems. In this sense, an activity system is a virtual disturbance – and innovation – producing engine (Engeström, 2001). In the following section, the emergence of contradictions, as well as the four types of contradictions, will be explained in more detail.

An activity system interacts with a network of other activity systems: it receives instruments and rules from other activity systems (e.g., regulatory agencies) and produces outcomes for certain other activity systems (e.g., clients). Influences from the outside 'intrude' into activity systems. However, such external forces are not a sufficient explanation for changes in the activity. Outside influences are first turned and modified into internal forces. Causation occurs as the alien element becomes internal to the activity; the system becomes imbalanced and contradictions emerge.

The primary contradiction of activities in capitalist socio-economic formations is that between the use value and the exchange value of commodities. The work activity of a medical doctor may serve as an illustration. The primary contradiction in object of the doctor's work activity takes the form of patient as 'person to be healed' versus patient as 'source of revenue'. The primary contradiction is also present in the instruments of the doctor: the tremendous variety of medicaments and drugs are not just useful for healing, but are above all commodities with prices, advertised and sold for profit.

When an activity system adopts a new element from the outside (e.g., a new technology or a new object) this often leads to secondary contradictions between the elements, where some old element (e.g., the rules or the division of labour) collides with a new one. Such contradictions generate disturbances and conflicts, but also innovative attempts to change the activity. For example, conflicts may emerge between the increasingly complex symptoms of the patients and the traditional biomedical instruments, as patients' problems often do not comply with the standards of classical diagnosis and classification of diseases.

A tertiary contradiction appears when a culturally more advanced object and motive are generated or designed and introduced into the activity. The new ideas may be formally implemented, but they are internally resisted by the logic of the old activity. Quaternary contradictions are contradictions that emerge in inter-action between the changing central activity and its neighbouring activities. Suppose that a medical doctor, working on a new holistic and integrated basis, refers the patient to a hospital operating strictly on a traditional biomedical model. Conflicts and misunderstandings easily emerge between these activity systems.

The four types of contradictions characterised above may now be placed in a network of human activity systems (Figure 9.4).

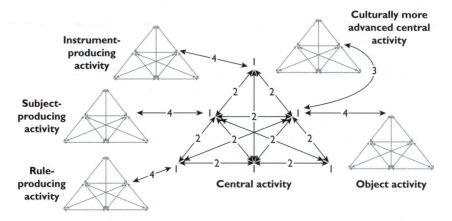

Figure 9.4 Four levels of contradictions in a network of human activity systems (Engeström, 1987, p. 89).

- *Level 1*: Primary inner contradiction within each element of the central activity.
- *Level 2*: Secondary contradictions between the constituents of the central activity.
- *Level 3*: Tertiary contradictions between the object/motive of the dominant form of the central activity and the object/motive of a culturally more advanced form of the central activity.
- *Level 4*: Quaternary contradictions between the central activity and its neighbour activities.

The fifth principle of activity theory proclaims the possibility of expansive transformations in activity systems. Because new qualitative forms of activity emerge as solutions to the contradictions of the preceding form, activity systems move through relatively long cycles of qualitative transformations. As the contradictions of an activity system are aggravated, some individual participants begin to question and deviate from its established norms. This may escalate into collaborative creating of a shared vision and a deliberate collective change effort. An expansive transformation is accomplished when the object and motive of the activity are reconceptualised to embrace a radically wider horizon of possibilities than in the previous mode of the activity. A full cycle of expansive transformation may be understood as a collective journey through the zone of proximal development of the activity: 'it is the distance between the current everyday actions of the individuals and the new form of the societal activity that can be collectively generated as a solution to the double bind potentially embedded in the everyday actions' (Engeström, 1987, p. 174).

Expansive learning as a way of producing new forms of work activity

Standard theories of learning focus on processes where an individual or an organisation acquires knowledge that is reasonably stable and well defined. In organisations it is very often the case that what is to be learned is given from above, from the management. Yet, individuals and organisations learn continuously something that is unstable, poorly defined or not even understood ahead of time. Important transformations often involve learning of forms of activity that are not yet there. They are literally learned as they are being created.

Traditional modes of learning deal with tasks in which the contents to be learned are well known ahead of time by those who create and run various programmes of learning. When whole activity systems, such as organisations, need to redefine themselves, such traditional modes of learning are not sufficient (Engeström & Sannino, 2010). Moreover, at least two other recent factors add weight to the societal need for expansive learning. First, the emergence and escalation of social production or peer production through social networking using the Internet opens up many possibilities for the formation of new types of activities. Second, the emergence of global threats and risks, or 'runaway objects' (Engeström, 2008), for example global warming, new pandemic diseases, global financial disasters or global drinkable water problems, opens up a field of tremendous challenges for concept formation and practical redesign on a scale that has to exceed the boundaries of any single discipline, profession or organisation (Engeström & Sannino, 2010).

Theories that do make a distinction between adaptive learning and innovative or creative learning do not pay enough attention to empirical elaboration of how the real learning happens. If innovative and creative learning is so important to organisational development, it should be observed and analysed more specifically (Engeström, 2004).

Expansive learning does not eliminate or replace other forms of learning. Two conceptualisations have been helpful in characterising expansive learning in relation to more traditional forms of learning. The first is Bateson's (1972) theory of levels of learning. The second is a matrix of four types of learning at work (Engeström, 2004).

Bateson's theory of learning distinguishes between three levels of learning: Learning I, II and III. Learning I refers to conditioning, the acquisition of responses that are considered correct in a specific context. Learning I can happen through reinforcement by rewards and punishments and it can be incidental and tacit. The learning of correct answers in a classroom would be an example of such conditioning. According to Bateson, where Learning I happens, Learning II is also going on. People acquire rules and patterns of behaviour characteristic to the context itself – they learn the rules of the game, so to speak. For example, students learn the 'hidden curriculum' of what it means to be a student: how to please the teachers; how to pass exams; how to belong to groups; etc. Sometimes Learning II creates a double bind, meaning that the participants face contradictory demands. The demands or messages from their environment seem so contradictory that they just do not know what to do. This can lead to a virtual paralysis, but it can also trigger Learning III, in which a person or a group begins to radically question the sense and meaning of the present context and to construct a wider alternative context. They, in a way, distance themselves from the given context to construct a bigger picture, to expand the picture. Engeström calls Learning III expansive learning, but develops it further by constructing a systematic conceptual framework (Engeström, 1987).

Another conceptualisation is a matrix of four ways of learning. Four types of learning are identified by constructing two dimensions: (1) given versus newly emerging nature of the object and activity that the learning serves; and (2) exploitation of existing knowledge versus exploration for new knowledge (Figure 9.5).

The exploitation of existing knowledge and skills can be analysed as transferable or adjustable. In transferable exploitation the existing knowledge is transferred in order to handle the new object and new activity. In adjustable exploitation existing knowledge is gradually acquired and internalised. Exploration for new knowledge can be acquired through incremental or radical exploration. Incremental exploration is the construction of new knowledge in the existing activity, whereas in radical

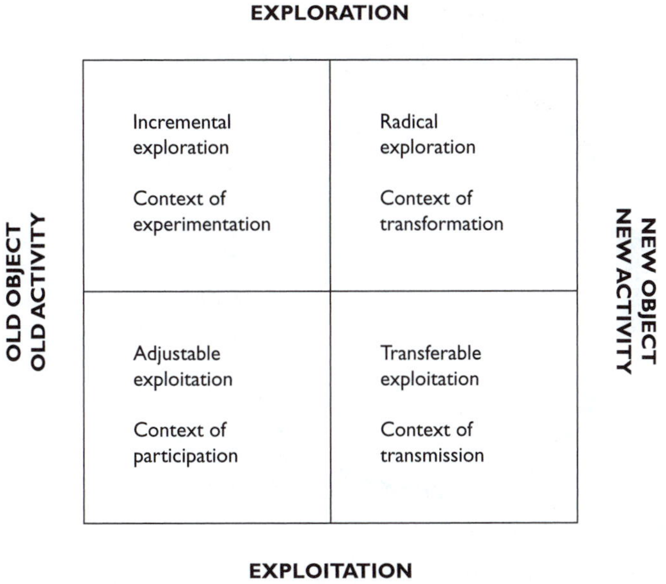

EXPLORATION

	Incremental exploration Context of experimentation	Radical exploration Context of transformation	
OLD OBJECT OLD ACTIVITY	Adjustable exploitation Context of participation	Transferable exploitation Context of transmission	**NEW OBJECT NEW ACTIVITY**

EXPLOITATION

Figure 9.5 Four types of learning (based on Engeström, 2004, p. 14).

exploration, or expansive learning also, the activity and object are reconstructed. Expansive learning processes include layers of the other processes, but in that case they gain a different meaning, motive and perspective (Engeström, 2004).

Expansive learning can be described as the construction of new forms of collaborative practice through the resolution of contradictions that the activity system faces. Learning is regarded as a stepwise, collaborative construction of new forms of practice. The expansive cycle begins when individuals start to question the existing practice, and it gradually expands into a collective movement (Engeström, 1999).

Central here is the dialectics of ascending from the abstract to the concrete. The ascension from abstract to concrete is achieved through specific learning actions. At the same time the cycle evolves continually, producing new theoretical concepts. Together these actions form an expansive cycle or spiral. An ideal-typical sequence of learning actions in an expansive cycle is depicted in Figure 9.6. As pointed out by Engeström and Sannino (2010, p. 7), 'the "what" of expansive learning consists of a triplet: expanded pattern of activity, corresponding theoretical concept, and new type of agency'.

The cycle of expansive learning can be considered as a theoretical generalisation of how new activity emerges in a working community. The cycle is also used as a foundation for research and work development in developmental work research interventions (Engeström, Lompscher, & Rückriem, 2005). In a developmental work research project, a researcher or the coordinator is helping the organisation

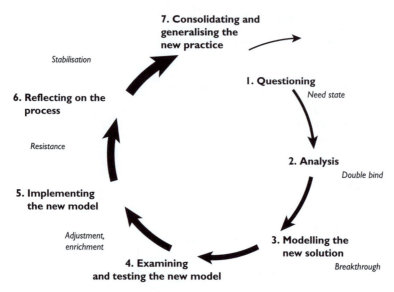

Figure 9.6 Sequence of learning actions in an expansive learning cycle (Engeström, 1999, p. 384).

to 'push' the development of activity forward on the expansive cycle. Typically, employees of the organisation participate closely in the process as analysts and designers of their own work. The theory of expansive learning has been applied mainly to demanding transformations that might take two to three years. We will now describe the phases of the expansive cycle in detail, paying particular attention to its uses as a tool in developmental work research interventions (see Engeström, 1999; Virkkunen, Engeström, Helle, & Pihlaja, 1999).

1   *The action of questioning.* The first action of the expansive learning cycle includes questioning, criticising or rejecting some aspects of the accepted and existing knowledge and practices. When the expansive cycle is used as a framework for the development of work, this phase corresponds to the ethnography of current problems. Notable here is to realise the multi-voicedness of the activity system: not all participants see the situation in the same way; their points of view may collide. Ethnographic data can be obtained by observing, interviewing, videotaping critical tasks and interactions within the activity and collecting documents.

2   *The action of analysis.* The second action is to analyse the history of the activity system and its current contradictions. Analysis includes mental, discursive, or practical transformation of the situation in order to find out causes or explanatory mechanisms. Analysis evokes 'why' questions and explanatory principles.

This phase includes historical-genetic analysis: it seeks to explain the situation by tracing its origination and evolution. Historical analysis is important because new practices do not emerge out of a vacuum; they are always constructed on the basis of earlier activities and practices, as answers to contradictions in the activity system. Recognition of previous historical phases helps the work community to realise what kind of different 'layers' of activity – tools, rules, roles, etc. – there are and how these influence the current work. Another type of analysis is actual-empirical. Whereas historical analysis can provide only a draft of the current contradictions, the object of actual-empirical analysis is to explain the current situation by constructing a picture of its inner systemic relations. In short this means that a clearer picture is drawn about the contradictions that are affecting the current situation and generating troubles at work. Data can be collected by interviews, observing and recording strategic work phases and interactions or by 'work diaries' written by the employees.

3   *The action of modelling a new solution.* The aim of the third action is to create a new solution to the contradictions of the activity system. An explicit, very simple first model is created to offer a solution to the contradictions discovered in the previous analysis. Modelling may be facilitated by using metaphors or prototyping as springboards for the articulation of the new idea. The new model is enriched and made concrete in multiple iterations.

4   *The action of examining and testing the new model.* The new model is examined by running it in thought experiments, simulated situations and small-scale practical tests. Examining the model implies revising and improving, which often means returning to the action of modelling.

5   *The action of implementing the new model.* When the new model is implemented in actual practice, conflicts and tertiary contradictions typically emerge in the organisation as old and new action patterns collide. This phase is typically not quick and requires longitudinal follow-up and support. When implementation is taken seriously, it can produce crucially important enrichments and conceptual extensions to the new model.

6   *The action of reflecting on the process.* Expansive learning includes constant reflection and evaluation of the process by the participants. This includes assessing the outcomes: Has the new model proved to be a resolution to contradictions that earlier plagued the activity? Has the model been implemented as planned? Reflection and evaluation require longitudinal data that allow comparisons of the quality of the activity between different points in the cycle.

7   *The action of consolidating and generalising the new practice.* The stabilisation of a new form of activity typically requires diffusion and generalisation across multiple sites and tasks, as well as codification of new rules and procedures.

The expansive learning cycle and its actions should be seen as a theoretical generalisation of how something new is created. In reality, learning and development do not occur in a straightforward manner. There is always movement back and forth between the different actions. An initially expansive learning cycle can also be thwarted, fall apart, split into multiple directions or cease altogether.

New forms of expansive learning at work: learning for and in co-configuration

Several recent studies at CRADLE have focused on how learning happens in co-configuration settings. In short, the concept of co-configuration can be understood as a new way of organising work in settings where multiple, loosely interconnected parties (typically including the client or customer) operate collaboratively to produce adaptive, continuously customised customer-intelligent products or services. The theory of expansive learning can be used as a starting point for understanding how learning can happen within a setting like this. But, as the theory of expansive learning was initially developed to illuminate learning in single activity systems, the current research is also developing further the theory of expansive learning itself.

Victor and Boynton (1998) identify five types of work in the history of industrial production: craft; mass production; process enhancement; mass customisation; and co-configuration (Figure 9.7). Depending on the type of work, different types of knowledge and learning are required and generated (Engeström, 2004, 2008; Victor & Boynton, 1998).

For co-configuration work to be successful, dialogue and renegotiation of collaborative relations and practices between different parties becomes crucial. This is not an easy task. Usually different parties are loosely interconnected, they are operating in divided local and global terrains, their traditions, domains of expertise, language used, etc., can be different from each other. The work itself is about putting together products or services that are complex and have a long life cycle

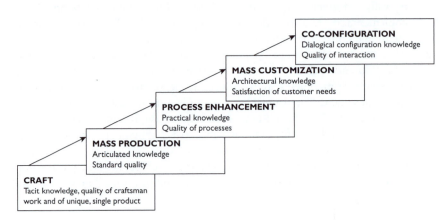

Figure 9.7 Historical forms of work (Engeström, 2004; modelled on Victor & Boynton, 1998).

(Engeström, 2004). Difficulties in carrying out co-configuration work can be described with a metaphor of playing a game:

> The actors are like blind players who come eagerly to the field in the middle of the game, attracted by shouting voices, not knowing who else is there and what the game is all about. There is no referee, so rules are made up in different parts of the field among those who happen to bump into one another. Some get tired and go home.
>
> (Kangasoja, 2002, in Engeström, 2003, p. 3)

Learning in co-configuration can be considered as a twofold challenge: first, the organisations working in this kind of setting need to learn co-configuration work itself, this is learning for co-configuration. Here, expansive learning takes the shape of renegotiation and reorganisation of collaborative interactions and practices. It also takes the form of creating and implementing concepts, tools, rules and infrastructures for such practices. Second, the parties involved in co-configuration need to learn constantly from interactions in co-configuration – that would be from the user, the product or service and the producers. And as the product of co-configuration work is never actually finished but is continuously customised, the very nature of co-configuration work can be seen as expansive (Engeström, 2004).

Co-configuration work requires flexible knotworking. The notion of knotworking implies that no single actor has a sole fixed authority about the activity: the centre does not hold. Different people take the initiative at different times, there are no fixed teams; the continuity of the activity is dependent on the power of the shared object and tools. Knots differ from teams or project groups which have a fixed membership for a specific period of time; knots are constituted by individuals and groups from interacting organisations (e.g., hospitals, schools or law courts) who meet flexibly for short periods to resolve particular challenging problems. Moreover, unlike teams where leadership and membership are usually fixed in advance, the locus of initiative changes from moment to moment within a knotworking sequence as members of interacting multiple teams and their clients engage in inter-professional collaboration (ibid., p. 153).

Another term often used to describe co-configuration work is boundary crossing. Boundary crossing means interaction and movement across the formal boundaries of different activity systems. This can occur in the form of negotiation, trading of information, etc. Boundary crossing has been a useful concept in studies of new forms of collaboration between institutions of vocational education and workplaces (Tuomi-Gröhn & Engeström, 2003).

Lambert (1999, 2003) examined boundary crossing in the field of vocational teacher education. Traditional teacher education tends to take the standard practices of classroom teaching for granted. The culmination of Finnish vocational teacher education has been the 'proof lesson' given by the student teacher to demonstrate his or her ability to teach in practice. In such a model, the new challenges and development efforts of the work organisations that eventually employ the students of vocational education are all but completely absent. Teacher education is an encapsulated world of its own. Lambert replaced the proof lessons with a boundary-crossing arena called Learning Studio. The student teachers were asked to conduct development projects in the workplaces, aimed at improving their teaching practices. Each student teacher presented a report of his or her project in the Learning Studio. In the Learning Studio, participants included representatives of the teacher education institute, teachers and students of the vocational training school in which the student teacher worked and representatives of employer organisations. The participants discussed the student teacher's project as a possible shared innovation and as a crossing of multiple boundaries. This resulted in the reciprocal exchange and adoption of ideas driven by a shared, potentially expansive object – a process called developmental transfer. Lambert found that successful boundary crossing and developmental transfer were largely dependent on the employment of appropriate tools such as forms, knowledge repositories and graphic models that played an important role in the expansion of the shared object. As can be hypothesised, theory and knowledge about team learning is closely related to the concept of boundary crossing, and can fertilise further ideas related to expansive learning (Decuyper, Dochy, & Van den Bossche, 2010).

Application in practice: children's medical care in Finland

The theory of expansive learning has been used in studies exploring learning, for example in telecommunications and media companies, post offices, farms and agricultural networks, industrial plants, health care and social welfare organisations, and of course various educational institutions. Most of the studies have involved developmental or formative interventions. Here we will give a condensed example of a longitudinal study of children's medical care in Helsinki (see Engeström, 2001). In this case, the theory of expansive learning was utilised in the form of Change Laboratory intervention sessions. Change Laboratory is an intervention method developed at CRADLE in the early 1990s. Change Laboratory aims to speed up and intensify the cycle of expansive learning and to develop new forms of activity to handle the emerging contradictions.

The public health care services in Finland are mainly funded by taxation, and patients usually only pay a nominal fee for their care. The problem is that approximately 15 per cent of the patients use almost 80 per cent of all resources. One of the most critical patient groups is children with long-term illnesses, especially those with multiple diagnoses. Many of these patients are so expensive for the health care system, in part because they drift from one caregiver to another and nobody has an overall responsibility for their care. This also puts a heavy burden on the family. In the mid-1990s, the Children's Hospital in Helsinki decided to respond to these pressures by initiating and hosting a collaborative redesign effort, facilitated by a research group using the Change Laboratory method. Approximately 60 physicians, nurses, other staff and management from primary care health centres and hospitals responsible for children's health care in Helsinki met in ten three-hour sessions.

The learning challenge was to acquire a new way of working in which parents and different caregiver organisations would collaboratively plan and monitor the child's trajectory of care, taking joint responsibility for its overall progress. There was no readily available model that would fix the problems. The issue at stake was organisational, not resolvable by a sum total of separate individuals. On the other hand, there was no mythical collective subject that could be approached and pushed to take charge of the transformation. Top-down commands and guidelines are of little value when the management does not know what the content of such directives should be. In this case, learning needs to occur in a changing mosaic of interconnected activity systems: the activity systems of the Children's Hospital; the health centre; and the child's family. In each particular patient case, the specific instantiation of these three main activity systems is different.

In the Change Laboratory sessions participants met face to face and articulated the contradictory demands inherent in their work activity by presenting a series of troublesome patient cases captured on videotape. The cases demonstrated in various ways that problems were caused by lack of coordination and communication between the different care providers. This invoked questioning. In several sessions, the patient's mother was also present. This made it virtually impossible for the participants to blame the clients for the problems and added greatly to the urgency of the double bind where the current state is clearly seen as intolerable. The practitioners did also begin to produce questioning actions in their own voices. This led to analyses of the cases, and eventually to sharper and more articulated questioning. The analysis of contradictions culminated later and was manifested as a conflict between the existing tools (normative disease-specific care pathways) and the new object (patients with multiple and interacting chronic illnesses). Out of these debates, a new direction began to emerge.

Initial suggestions towards modelling a new solution were formulated in terms of 'care negotiations' between the various caregivers. These ideas were first rejected as requiring too much extra work and resources. The critical discussion and rejection of this proposal is an example of the action of examining the new model. A more carefully designed model called 'care agreement'(see Figure 9.8) slowly started to emerge in the sessions, but it was still discussed in parallel with the old model of disease-specific care pathways. The new model was worked out in more detail, but did not become fully accepted before the last session.

The basic idea of the care agreement is fourfold. First, the patient's personal physician in the health centre is designated as the coordinator in charge of the patient's network and trajectory of care across institutional boundaries. Second, whenever a child becomes a patient of the Children's Hospital for more than a single visit, the hospital physician and nurse in charge of the child draft a care agreement which includes a plan for the patient's care and the division of labour between the different care providers contributing to the care of the child. The

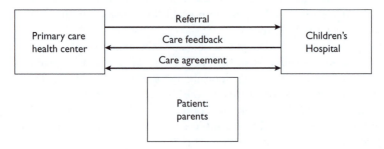

Figure 9.8 The conceptual model of the care agreement practice (Engeström, 2001, p. 149).

draft agreement is given to the child's family and sent to the child's personal health centre physician for their scrutiny. Third, if one or more of the parties find it necessary, they will have a care negotiation (by e-mail, by telephone or face to face) to formulate a mutually acceptable care agreement. Fourth, care feedback, in the form of a copy of the patient's medical record, is given automatically and without delay or sent to the other parties of the care agreement after the patient's unplanned visit or changes in diagnoses or care plans. The care agreement can be described as a flexible combination of contracts, where the centre will change with every new patient.

In this case, inter-organisational knotworking for coordinated and collaborative care was the central learning challenge. Subsequent research (Kerosuo, 2006; Saaren-Seppälä, 2004) shows that in spite of the successful creation of a new model, implementation, diffusion and consolidation of the new practice in the scale of the city and health care district were not successful. Much more research and development is needed for the understanding and effective facilitation of these later actions of the expansive learning cycle.

Another application: sustainable agriculture in Africa

A question frequently asked about expansive learning concerns its applicability across cultures. Can expansive learning take place among people with relatively weak educational backgrounds and in non-industrial, non-Western contexts? A recent study by Mukute (2010) on expansive learning processes aimed at supporting sustainable agricultural practices in three African countries is a powerful answer to this question.

Mukute conducted a Change Laboratory in each of the three sites, each involved in a specific variant of sustainable agriculture. Participants of the Change Laboratory sessions included sustainable agriculture farmers, sustainable agriculture facilitators, extension workers and organic marketers. Figure 9.9 summarises the actual course of expansive learning in one of Mukute's three sites.

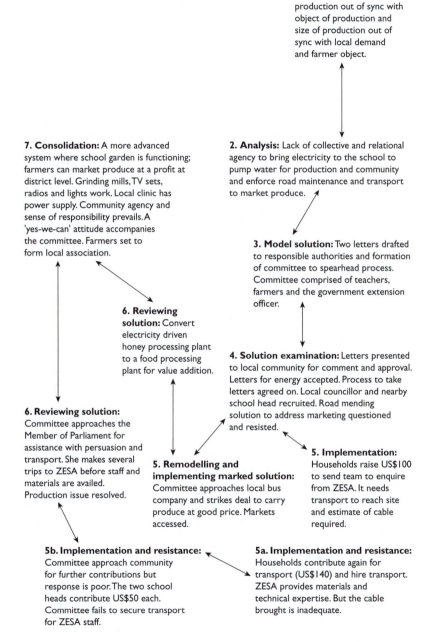

1. Contradiction: Means of production out of sync with object of production and size of production out of sync with local demand and farmer object.

7. Consolidation: A more advanced system where school garden is functioning; farmers can market produce at a profit at district level. Grinding mills, TV sets, radios and lights work. Local clinic has power supply. Community agency and sense of responsibility prevails. A 'yes-we-can' attitude accompanies the committee. Farmers set to form local association.

2. Analysis: Lack of collective and relational agency to bring electricity to the school to pump water for production and community and enforce road maintenance and transport to market produce.

3. Model solution: Two letters drafted to responsible authorities and formation of committee to spearhead process. Committee comprised of teachers, farmers and the government extension officer.

6. Reviewing solution: Convert electricity driven honey processing plant to a food processing plant for value addition.

4. Solution examination: Letters presented to local community for comment and approval. Letters for energy accepted. Process to take letters agreed on. Local councillor and nearby school head recruited. Road mending solution to address marketing questioned and resisted.

6. Reviewing solution: Committee approaches the Member of Parliament for assistance with persuasion and transport. She makes several trips to ZESA before staff and materials are availed. Production issue resolved.

5. Remodelling and implementing marked solution: Committee approaches local bus company and strikes deal to carry produce at good price. Markets accessed.

5. Implementation: Households raise US$100 to send team to enquire from ZESA. It needs transport to reach site and estimate of cable required.

5b. Implementation and resistance: Committee approach community for further contributions but response is poor. The two school heads contribute US$50 each. Committee fails to secure transport for ZESA staff.

5a. Implementation and resistance: Households contribute again for transport (US$140) and hire transport. ZESA provides materials and technical expertise. But the cable brought is inadequate.

Figure 9.9 Expansive learning process in Mukute's first case study (2010, p. 271).

Three features stand out in Figure 9.9. First, the actions of expansive learning are described in vivid detail and concreteness. They may look like small and insignificant local struggles. But they led to a foundational change in the infra-structural resources (electricity) and in the actual object and substance of the production (from honey processing to food processing). Simultaneously the expansive learning cycle led to collective agency, including the formation of a local association of farmers.

Second, the expansive learning process in this case involved negotiations across boundaries, primarily between the committee of local practitioners and the powerful electricity company ZESA but also with such actors as the Member of Parliament. Mukute summarises this field of knotworking connections as follows:

> . . . the research participants exercised their agency by engaging with structures and systems of local governance (councillors and headmasters), the district political head (Member of Parliament), ZESA (quasi-government), the NGO which constructed the honey processing plant (civil society) and the corporate sector (bus company). The agency, which lay 'dormant' in them, was activated through engagement in the Change Laboratory workshop.
>
> (Ibid., p. 273)

Third, the sequence of expansive learning actions was not at all linear and orderly. The actions of implementation and reflection (reviewing) particularly took shape as virtual iterative mini-cycles, with multi-directional feedback loops. Despite this, all the crucial elements of expansive learning could be identified and their overall shape is not so chaotic after all.

Arguably the most important outcome of expansive learning is agency – participants' ability and will to shape their activity systems (Engeström & Sannino, 2010; Virkkunen, 2006). A major challenge for the study of expansive learning is to conceptualise and characterise empirically the new forms of agency involved in expansive processes. In his study, Mukute took an important step in this direction. Using Sannino's (2008) study of forms of agentive talk as his starting point, Mukute analysed in detail the discourse in his three interventions. He identified a rich repertoire of agentive talk sequences, including sequences of suggesting that something is doable (optimistic talk), sequences of envisioning new models and sequences of commissive talk (committing to specific action). He also found that metaphors were repeatedly used 'as a strategy of meaning-making, used to persuade each other to act' (Mukute, 2010, p. 312).

Conclusions

Activity theory and the theory of expansive learning are complex frameworks. In these theories, learning and development are seen both as something slowly evolving but then again as something that people can make happen. New activity does not just emerge from nowhere. It is developed from the contradictions of old activity. Developmental work research based on these two theories not only offers new methodological tools for organisational learning and development – such as the Change Laboratory – but also new conceptual tools, such as knot-working and boundary crossing.

Are activity theory and the theory of expansive learning too complicated to really be an option for work development in organisations? Their implementation does require quite a lot from the participants. If this kind of developmental process is initiated in an organisation where severe problems are hampering the work, can it really work? Do the individuals in such a situation really have the energy to go through all the analysis and discussions? And if the process of expansive learning takes two or three years, what happens if the employee turnover is high?

Another issue that might hinder the use of these theories in work development is that it requires deep understanding of the theories. So, if the organisation does not have internal resources to educate someone in this methodology, they will need an outsider to coordinate the process, i.e., an expert in the Change Laboratory method. And if an outsider is used, what happens after this outsider leaves? The theory also implies that the organisation should be open enough so that questioning – which is the starting point of expansive learning – is accepted and encouraged. If this is not the case, can expansive learning still happen?

Mukute's study introduced above seems like a good initial response to these questions:

> The expansive learning process helped participants to develop model solutions to some of the problems they are facing in workplaces, including the invisible dimensions. They appreciated the expansive learning process and are likely to work with these processes of collaborative engagement beyond the intervention workshops. This was evidenced by the processes that took place in each case study between the first Change Laboratory workshop and the feedback meetings and workshops that occurred several months later.
>
> (Ibid., p. 292)

Revisiting 'Tourism for everyone!'

The case study of the learning network of 'Holiday Participation' can be seen as a 'real life' application of the theory of inter-organisational expansive learning. Many organisations participate, each of them confronted with contradictions related to 'a need for some holidays' versus 'being poor'. They bring in different voices and cultures, they participate in the planned activities and, through knot-working in different knots during different meetings, they take on new challenges, they cross boundaries and they come to new solutions. As such, organisations redefine themselves by means of expansive learning. The focus of the meetings was to learn from each other's good practices, promoting partnerships and creating new ways of handling challenges in working with this target group. The network collaboratively created a shared vision that can be seen as an example of the result of knotworking. This knotworking took place through different activities, and profited from boundary crossing through interaction between organisations from the profit and non-profit sectors. New solutions for upcoming contradictions were designed out of shared understanding of practices.

References

Bateson, G. (1972). *Steps to an ecology of mind*. New York: Ballantine Books.

Decuyper, S., Dochy, F., & Van den Bossche, P. (2010). 'Grasping the dynamic complexity of team learning. An integrative model for effective team learning in organisations', *Educational Research Review*, 5(2), 111–133.

Engeström, Y. (1987). *Learning by expanding: An activity-theoretical approach to developmental research*. Helsinki: Orienta-Konsultit.

Engeström, Y. (1999). 'Innovative learning in work teams: Analyzing cycles of knowledge creation in practice', in Y. Engeström, R. Miettinen, & R. L. Punamäki (eds), *Perspectives on activity theory* (pp. 377–404). Cambridge: Cambridge University Press.

Engeström, Y. (2000). 'From individual action to collective activity and back: Developmental work research as an interventionist methodology', in P. Luff, J. Hindmarsh, & C. Heath (eds), *Workplace studies* (pp. 150–166). Cambridge: Cambridge University Press.

Engeström, Y. (2001). 'Expansive learning at work: Toward an activity theoretical reconceptualization', *Journal of Education and Work*, 14(1), 133–155.

Engeström, Y. (2003). 'The horizontal dimension of expansive learning: Weaving a texture of cognitive trails in the terrain of health care in Helsinki', in F. Achtenhagen & E. G. John (eds), *Milestones of vocational and occupational education and training. Volume 1: The teaching-learning perspective* (pp. 153–180). Bielefeld: Bertelsmann.

Engeström, Y. (2004). 'New forms of learning in co-configuration work', *Journal of Workplace Learning*, 16(1/2), 11–21.

Engeström, Y. (2005). 'Knotworking to create collaborative intentionality capital in fluid organizational fields', in M. M. Beyerlein, S. T. Beyerlein, & F. A. Kennedy (eds), *Collaborative capital: Creating intangible value* (pp. 307–336). Amsterdam: Elsevier.

Engeström, Y. (2008). *From teams to knots: Activity-theoretical studies of collaboration and learning at work*. Cambridge: Cambridge University Press.

Engeström, Y., & Miettinen, R. (1999). 'Introduction', in Y. Engeström, R. Miettinen, & R. L. Punamäki (eds), *Perspectives on activity theory* (pp. 1–8). Cambridge: Cambridge University Press.

Engeström, Y., & Sannino, A. (2010). 'Studies of expansive learning: Foundations, findings and future challenges', *Educational Research Review*, 5, 1–24.

Engeström, Y., Lompscher, J., & Rückriem, G. (eds) (2005). *Putting activity theory to work: Contributions from developmental work research*. Berlin: Lehmanns Media.

Kangasoja, J. (2002). 'Complex design problems: An impetus for learning and knotworking', in P. Bell, R. Stevens, & T. Satwicz (eds), *Keeping learning complex: The proceedings of the fifth international conference on learning societies* (pp. 199–205). Mahwah, NJ: Erlbaum.

Kerosuo, H. (2006). *Boundaries in action: An activity-theoretical study of development, learning and change in health care for patients with multiple and chronic illnesses*. Helsinki: University of Helsinki, Department of Education.

Lambert, P. (1999). *Rajaviiva katoaa: Innovatiivista oppimista ammatillisen opettajankoulutuksen, oppilaitosten ja työelämän organisaatioiden yhteistyönä*

[*Boundaries fade away: Innovative learning through collaboration between vocational teacher education, training institutes, and work organizations*]. Helsinki: Helsingin ammattikorkeakoulu (in Finnish).

Lambert, P. (2003). 'Promoting developmental transfer in vocational teacher education', in T. Tuomi-Gröhn & Y. Engeström (eds), *Between school and work: New perspectives on transfer and boundary crossing* (pp. 233–254). Amsterdam: Pergamon.

Leont'ev, A. N. (1978). *Activity, consciousness, and personality*. Englewood Cliffs, NJ: Prentice-Hall.

Leont'ev, A. N. (1981). *Problems of the development of the mind*. Moscow: Progress.

Mukute, M. (2010). 'Exploring and expanding learning processes in sustainable agriculture workplace contexts', Ph.D. thesis. Grahamstown, South Africa: Rhodes University.

Roth, W.-M., & Lee, Y.-J. (2007). 'Vygotsky's neglected legacy: Cultural-historical activity theory', *Review of Educational Research*, 77(2), 186–232.

Saaren-Seppälä, T. (2004). *Yhteisen potilaan hoito: Tutkimus organisaatiorajat ylittävästä yhteistoiminnasta sairaalan, terveyskeskuksen ja lapsipotilaiden vanhempien suhteissa* [*The care of a shared patient: A study of collaboration across organizational boundaries between hospital, health center and parents of child patients*]. Tampere: University of Tampere (in Finnish).

Sannino, A. (2008). 'From talk to action: Experiencing interlocution in developmental interventions', *Mind, Culture, and Activity*, 15, 234–257.

Sfard, A. (1998). 'On two metaphors of learning and the dangers of choosing just one', *Educational Researcher*, 27(2), 4–13.

Tuomi-Gröhn, T., & Engeström, Y. (eds) (2003). *Between school and work: New perspectives on transfer and boundary crossing*. Amsterdam: Pergamon.

Victor, B., & Boynton, A. (1998). *Invented here: Maximizing your organization's internal growth and profitability. A practical guide to transforming work*. Boston, MA: Harvard Business School Press.

Virkkunen, J. (2006). 'Hybrid agency in co-configuration work', *Outlines*, 8(1), 61–75.

Virkkunen, J., Engeström, Y., Helle, M., & Pihlaja, J. (1999). *Muutoslaboratorio: Uusi tapa oppia ja kehittää työtä* [*The Change Laboratory: A new way to learn and develop work practice*]. Helsinki: Ministry of Labour (in Finnish).